# Miles Around The World Vol. 1

*By* Shawn Miles

# Miles Around The World Vol. 1

## *By Shawn Miles*

Miles Around The World: Recipes I created, based on places I've Been. By Shawn Miles

Published by A Little Brit Different LLC

Foreword by Brannon Taylor

ISBN: 9780578981710

[Vol 1] First Edition

# Dedication

*This book is dedicated to my late father, Harold Miles. My father was the one that taught me to have an open mind when it comes to food. There wasn't a food he hadn't tried if he had the opportunity! I credit him with many things but my love for all types of foods stems from him. Rest In Peace!*

In Loving memory
of my father,
Harold Miles.

# CONTENTS

FOREWORD

INTRODUCTION

DRINKS
JUNGLE JUICE
SANGRIA
WOO GAL
BEER COLA
ENERGY DRINK SPLASH
COGNAC & PINEAPPLE
YUMMY BEARS
COFFEEADE

SIDE DISHES
LEEK SOUP
HOT WINGS
BACON WRAPPED GREEN BEANS
CORNBREAD DRESSING
DRESSING WAFFLE
BACKED PASTA AND CHEESE
BUTTERNUT SQUASH SOUP
SAVOURY BUTTERNUT SQUASH
BUTTERNUT SQUASH RISOTTO
4 STAR MEATBALLS

WEDDING SOUP
BLACK BEANS
AVOCADO TOAST
WHITE BEAN DITALINI SOUP
LOBSTER QUESADILLAS
POTATO RÖSTI

GRILLING AND CHILLIN'
BASIC BBQ DRY RUB
BRISKET
PORK BUTT
SMOKED RIBS
BALCONY STEAKS
SCHWENKBRATEN
BBQ CHICKEN
BAKED BEANS
YAKITORI

# CONTENTS

## MAINS

ZÜRCHER GESCHNETZETZELTES

BEER BRATS

CHEESY EGG DROP RAMEN

SLOW COOKER BARBACOA

RAHMSNITZEL

WHITE BEAN CHICKEN CHILI

LASAGNA

CHOPPED CHEESE

TACO RICE

BEEF ENCHILADAS

SHRIMP & GRITS

FISH TACOS

CHICKEN KATSU CURRY

BRAISED OXTAILS

## SWEET THANGS

PECAN PIE

BAKLAVA

AÇAÍ BOWL

GRILLED PINEAPPLES

SALTED CARAMEL COGNAC ICE CREAM

COGNAC GLAZED PEACH TURNOVERS

## ACKNOWLEDGEMENTS AND THANK YOU'S

# Foreword

We all have our favorite foods or meals that we enjoy eating often and on special occasions. Those memories might be based on childhood memories, a first date, those college nights out with friends, holiday family meals, and meals had while on vacation. We often share these moments with friends and family through conversation, hoping they have the same or better experience you have enjoyed. We often return to the place to enjoy these meals, but how many of us try to cook them ourselves? We are all capable of whirling up foods we like to eat. We may think these meals are time consuming or just a tad past our comfort level in complexity.

I met Shawn in the United Kingdom some 20 years ago and he has always had a flair for creativity with his cooking. A great memory of mine with Shawn, was a few years after he left England. He took me to a local restaurant in Texas. We ordered our food and I was constantly going on about how good it tasted. He tells he can do it better. When we get the check, he asks the server what ingredients were used to prepare the meal. We leave the restaurant, and he goes to the grocery store and purchases the ingredients. He made the meal and added some spices and proved that he could make it better than the restaurant. It was!

# Foreword

He often spoke about creating a cookbook with more substance than a collection of recipes. Throughout his military career and years of travel, Shawn had cookouts and provided food for different occasions. The recipes he cooked came from his childhood and places all over the globe. All of the people who ate his meals loved his cooking. Like our favorite foods or meals, Shawn's recipes are from special occasions and moments at different points in his life. His desire to share his experiences detailed in this book provides a unique point of view, easy to follow recipes that are suited for any occasion.

I am sure we all agree that everyone likes to eat and not all of us like to cook! I think you will enjoy making these recipes and you will create new memories for your family and friends using this cookbook.

Shawn – Not all of us have a culinary talent that you possess, but thank you for the conversations, encouragement, and peer pressure in improving my cooking confidence!

*Brannon Taylor*

# Introduction

For as long as I can remember food has been a very important part of my life. My love of food sprung from watching my dad and mom make ordinary food come alive with techniques they learned from family members over the years. I never thought that food would hold such a sacred place in my heart until I got older.

Growing up I lived in a household with FOUR CHILDREN , OF WHICH I WAS THE YOUNGEST. MY FATHER WAS IN THE ARMY AND MY MOTHER WORKED FOR THE HOSPITAL IN THE LABOR AND DELIVERY ward. It was a rare occasion for us to eat pre-made food items. The main reason is the expensive cost of getting pre-cooked food. We had a tight budget and if our food wasn't made from scratch, we probably weren't going to be eating. You would be surprised how quick you can learn to cook when you are forced to make everything from scratch.

I used to get mad that I couldn't just shove a pack a pre-made pancakes in a microwave like some of my friends! No, if I wanted pancakes I had to get all of my ingredients ready and start cooking.

Little did I know that all of my frustrations would be the foundation for my love for food.

As mentioned earlier, my father was in the Army. I guess I fit the stereotypical profile of an Army Brat. Growing up I went to three different elementary schools, one middle school, and three different high schools. Change was a huge part of my upbringing! Being the son of a traveling solider had some advantages. I was fortunate to have friends that were all around the world, I got to see and experience new places, I met and had friends from multiple ethnic backgrounds and most importantly I was exposed to a bunch of different types of foods! My father was the person that would urge me to try new things that he had eaten over the years. He would tell me, "BOY STOP TURNIN' UP YOUR NOSE AND TRY IT". He drove a hard bargain, so I didn't argue too much! My father was from the South Side of Chicago, so his taste pallet was pretty well developed before he shipped off for the Army.

My mom on the other hand was raised in a small town called Richland, Georgia. Richland is one of those one stoplight type of towns. Honest hard working country folks. My mom would have to go out back and catch a chicken if she wanted fried chicken for dinner. She learned a lot from my grandmother about how to cook souther staples such as dressing(often mistaken for stuffing), fried chicken, collard greens, ext. The wide range in food pallets helped me develop my love for food at a young age.

# Introduction

Although I had a wide range of food knowledge at my disposal, I was rarely taught how to do anything in the kitchen. I would often get yelled at when I was in the kitchen because I was dirty from being outside or I was simply in the way. I have always had an inquisitive mind for as long as I can remember, so getting told to leave the kitchen wasn't gonna keep me from figuring out how to cook something I enjoyed.

I would sneak around and watch what my parents were doing while preparing meals in the kitchen. Whenever we had or went to a BBQ, kids were forbidden anywhere near the grill! I honestly had to be about 30 yards away from the grill when my dad or uncles were cooking. I still lurked in the shadows, sneaking a peak to see what I would do when I finally got my hands on a grill.

My first formal introduction to cooking was a Home Economics course that I took in 8th grade. I realized how much I knew about cooking, when I was amongst my peers. I caught on really quick and took a liking to being in the kitchen. I'll never forget how upset I was when my teams chili wasn't selected as the best in our Home EC chili cook off.

I began cooking a lot more when I started high school. My parents were divorced and my mother worked nights. By the time I got home from football practice, it was late at night. Some days my mom would cook before she went to work. Some days I had free range to do what I wanted in the kitchen. At first I burned a bunch of food, but I look at that as my crawling stage. This was long before I was putting together my own signature dishes.

My friends would come over my house and I would try new stuff that I learned and used them as taste testers. It wasn't hard to get a bunch of high school athletes to try free food!

Shortly after starting high school, one of my sisters put in a good word for me at the Chick-Fil-A she was a manager at. I was really excited that I was gonna get my chance at cooking in a professional style kitchen (also called "boards" at Chick-Fil-A). Little did I know, I was gonna have to work my way up to the boards section. Only the best employees were able to work the boards section at our store. Even though I wasn't able to work the boards section initially, I would ask questions and show up to work early so I could know how everything was done.

One day someone called out sick and I was given my shot to cook! Even though it was just fried chicken, I was amped up! I had been told my whole life, get out of the kitchen and now I was getting paid to cook for complete strangers! I felt like a chicken boss! I took pride in making the best food I could. I would taste everything we made and be very critical when things weren't

# Introduction

right. Chick-Fil-A has a great culture/quality standards and I credit them for making me demand more from the food I order.

When I was getting close to graduating high school, I couldn't decide what I wanted to do with my life. I knew I enjoyed cooking, but I wasn't interested in staying in Georgia and going to school.

I ended up getting a phone call from my local Air Force Recruiter. I forgot that I had taken an ASVAB test to get out of class. Apparently the Air Force was really looking for folks to come in as mechanics and I scored high in the mechanical area. Before I got that call from TSgt Dent, I had never really thought about going in the Air Force. I took a couple days to think it over and I felt joining the Air Force would help me explore the world (and food).

I ended up joining the Air Force and shipped out 2 months after I graduated high school. I haven't lived in Columbus,Ga since I shipped out.

My first assignment was in Okinawa, Japan. I was blown away by the different types of foods people ate in that part of the world. I started trying to break down what was in the foods I was eating, so that I could cook it for my friends and family at a later date.

My assignment to Okinawa was the catalyst that got me started on building recipes from all over the world. I was fortunate enough to have spent over 11 years of my 20 years in the Air Force overseas. I was able to try a bunch of different foods from a bunch of countries.

I came up with the idea of this cookbook based on an overwhelming response from my friends and family. I joked about making a cookbook with people that have eaten my food. Everyone that I joked about it would look me in the face and say "do it"!

I have been documenting things that I cook for years and I rarely eat the "typical" same foods that most people I know eat. I hope that people can read this book and get excited about food like I did when I was first given the reigns on the boards at Chick-Fil-A. I get that feeling every-time I am cooking for someone.

I came up with the title 'Miles Around The World" when I was talking with my sister about starting my own food truck. I thought it was a good play on words because my last name is Miles and I have been around the world, thanks to the Air Force. I am forever trying decipher new foods, so I can add to my stash of recipes.

I hope that you enjoy some of my favorite recipes, based off of places I have been or things that I grew up eating!

# CHAPTER 1
## Drinks

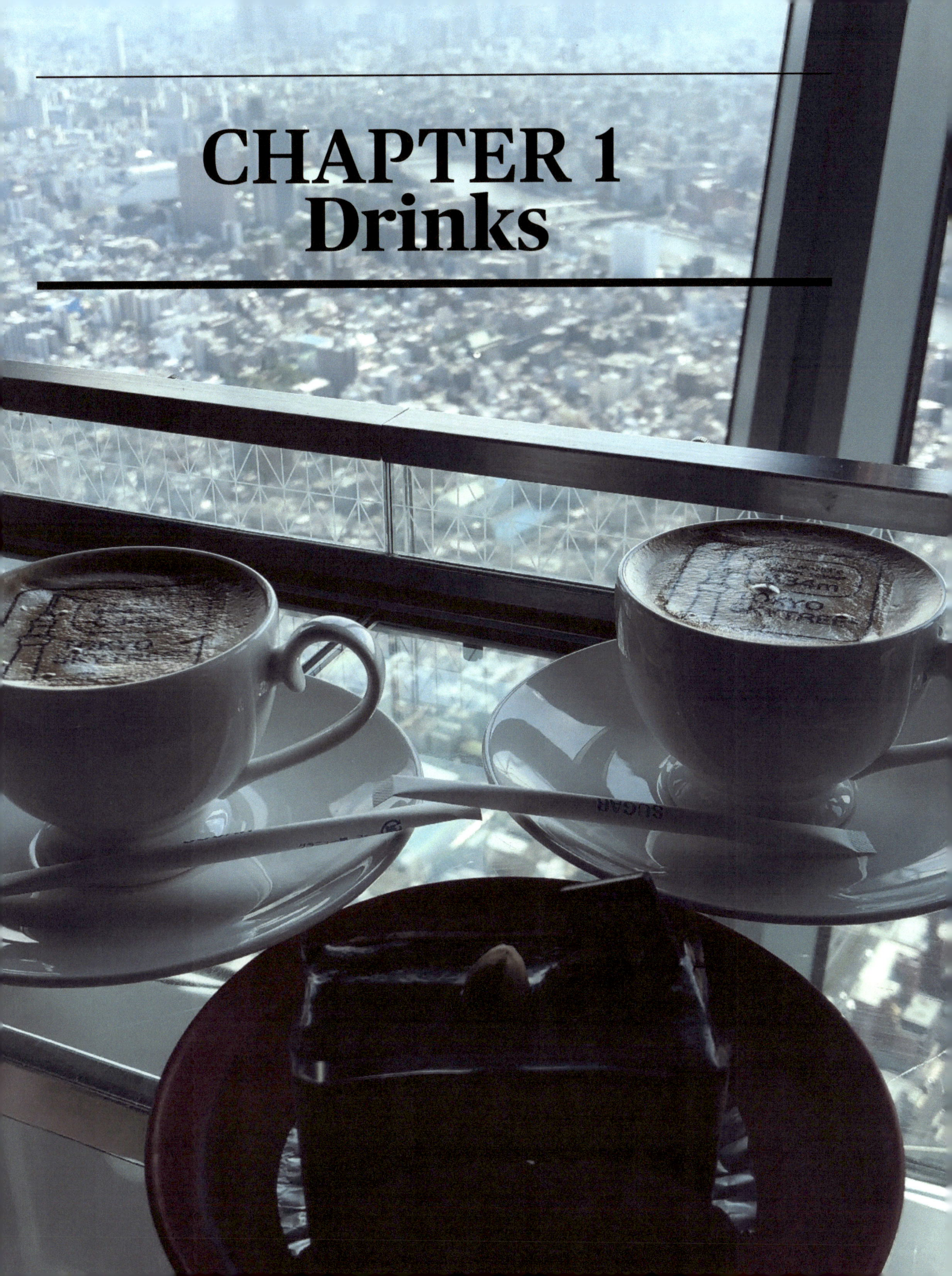

# DRINKS

- JUNGLE JUICE
- SANGRIA
- WOO GAL
- BEER COLA
- ENERGY DRINK SPLASH
- COGNAC AND PINEAPPLE
- YUMMY BEARS
- COFFEEADE

# Chapter 1
# Drinks

Nothing sets the mode quite like a pre meal drink. It doesn't matter if you are drinking water, a nice cocktail, tea or coffee. Drinks often help break the tension and get people talking. There is something magical about having a nice refreshing drink in front of you.

In this chapter I will share a few of my favorite drinks. All of the drinks have a special connection to some part of my life. Please enjoy responsibly!

Travel Tip:

Through my years of traveling, I've learned that the best place to get information about a town that you just landed in is at the bar. Bartenders are in a unique position where they get to talk to people that are tourists and locals. Bartenders often engage in conversation about all types of things that are happening locally. I think that tapping into the brains of bartenders is an invaluable source of information! It doesn't even matter if you like to drink alcoholic drinks. I have often ordered a soft drink at a bar just so I can speak with the bartender and get some intel about places to see in the local area. I'm not saying that you should avoid the concierge or information booths, I'm just saying don't pass up the chance to speak to a bartender.

My first base in the Air Force was Kadena Air Base. Kadena is located on the island of Okinawa in Japan. Okinawa is a beautiful island but when you are a long way from home and you are young, you get nostalgic for the things you know and miss. Most of the folks I hung around wanted to party and the Japanese tend to be more reserved than most Americans. We would have dorm parties on base whenever we could come up with enough funds. Most young Airmen that lived on base were down for a good dorm party because they were strapped for cash and dorm parties were cheaper than going out. I started DJ'ing when I was on Okinawa and I started hanging out with a bunch of other DJ's. We decided to start throwing dorm parties that were reminiscent of a good old fashion house party. The problem we ran into was trying to compete with other things that were going on, during the weekends.

The big question was "how can we get everyone to want to come to OUR party"? We knew we were spinning good music but we knew in order to get folks to come out we had to give them an incentive. We decided to give away free bottles of alcohol for the the person that could do the best_____ (insert bad idea and we probably did it). It was a crazy time. The problem with giving away free alcohol was, we didn't have a lot to go around for eager party goers. One of my buddies came up with the idea of getting a huge cooler (like we used when we were kids during sport practices) and fill it with jungle juice! I had never heard of "jungle juice" before. My friend said it is an alcoholic drink that is mixed with juice but you don't taste the alcohol!  I was down for this because it would accommodate a lot of people and wouldn't cost us a lot.

We pooled our money together, bought bottom shelf liquor and created one of the strongest drinks I have ever had in life! I told the guys that someone might die if they drank it because it was so strong! They weren't having it! In the back ground I hear a voice yelling " THE SHOW MUST GO ON". I said, "well if we are going to provide this at least let me make a sign to go on the cooler". I had a new computer and I really just wanted to show off my new "Word Art" skills if I'm being honest. I made a sign that said "1000 Proof Jungle Juice*" I put a disclaimer at the bottom behind an asterisk that said "drink at your own risk". Our first major dorm party was a success, and thankfully no one died from our Jungle Juice. Since that party, I have always kept Jungle juice as an option to provide a big group of people drinks. I will warn you that if you are going to make this or any form of this drink you need to be aware of who is consuming it and how much they drink. The smooth taste makes it go down really easy and the drink can sneak up on you very quick. I recommend having a day off and a designated driver in advance of consuming!

# Jungle Juice

**1 liter of lemon lime soda**

**1 gallon of Cranberry juice**

**2 cups of vodka**

**2 cups of rum**

**1 cup of triple sec**

**1 cup of peach schnapps**

**2 cups of Soju (optional)**

**Fresh sliced up fruit (oranges, kiwis, strawberries,& grapes)**

**Large drink cooler or container with a spout**

**Large bag of ice**

1.  In a large cooler mix all ingredients except ice and fruit with a large spoon. I use a cooler because it keeps ice from melting as fast.

2.  Once you have given your ingredients a good mix you will need to sample to make sure the mix is right. Ideally you don't want to be able to taste the alcohol that much.

3.  If you are satisfied with the flavor, mix in fruit and ice. I like to make the juice hours in advance to make sure the fruit has time to incorporate its flavors with the juice. Some of the ice will melt but I feel that the juice needs some of the water to even things out a bit.

4.  Give the cooler a good swirl every 30 minutes or so to help keep things nice and mixed.

5.  When your guest have arrived and you are ready to serve, bring your cooler out. Be sure to warn who ever is going to consume your jungle juice how strong it is! The last thing you need is someone's child thinking this is a normal punch drink!

6. This drink will sneak up on you if you are not careful, so please enjoy responsibly!

# Ibiza, Spain

Back in the early 2000's I was fortunate enough to book my first "real" vacation. I mean, up until this point I had been on a few trips here and there but I had never actually used a travel agent and booked a vacation abroad. I was stationed in German. I have to say I was kind of spoiled because I could drive to many places that some people spend thousands of dollars to vacation to. When I was trying to figure out where to go, I knew I wanted sun and fun.

I remembered I read an article that said that if you are into the club scene, then you must visit Ibiza before you die. I asked around until I found a friend willing to drop some money on a trip with me. Me and my friend were big into clubbing but we had no idea how hard they went in Ibiza, Spain.

We found a spot that we would plan out what clubs and bars we were going to hit up each day. We started every day at this cafe on the beach. The first day our waitress recommended that we have the Sangria. I had never had Sangria, so I said sure we'll have a pitcher. I was thinking to myself, "how bad can a pitcher of juice be"? Well, the waitress failed to mention that this "juice" was infused with many shots of liquor added to an already strong red wine base! You think we would have learned our lesson after the first pitcher. We didn't! In fact, we had a pitcher everyday while we were there. After asking our waitress on a daily basis what the recipe was, she finally caved and gave me a hint what was in it! I hope you enjoy my version of sangria inspired by my trip to Ibiza!

# Sangría

**Makes 1 Pitcher**

1  750ml bottle of red wine

2  large oranges

1 large apple

1 pear

1 lemon

1 cinnamon stick

1/2 cup of Cointreau

1 TBSP of sweetened lime juice

1/4 cup of Cognac or Brandy

1. Juice one of the large Oranges. The juice from your large orange should net you around 4-5 ounces of juice. Add the sweetened lime juice ( I like to use the Roses's brand) to your orange juice.

2.  Make sure that you thoroughly clean your fruit  because you will be leaving the skins and rinds on. Cut the remaining orange into slices. Cut your lemon into wedges or slices. Cut your apple and pear making sure to remove the core of each fruit.

3. Place all of your cut up fruit into a large glass pitcher. I like to use a glass pitcher because it will not stain and that is how it was served to me every time I order it in Spain.

4. Pour orange juice mixture over the fruit in the pitcher. Add in the whole bottle of red wine and the other portions of liquor in this recipe. Give the mixture a good stir with a wooden spoon. Add 1 whole cinnamon stick to the pitcher and over the top of the pitcher tightly with plastic kitchen wrap. The kitchen wrap will help keep any flavors from your refrigerator from tainting the taste of your Sangría. Place the pitcher in a refrigerator for at least 4 hours. I always wait until the next day before I try it.

5. When you are ready to serve place a few cubes of ice in a wide wine glass. Scoop out a few pieces of the fruit that has been soaking in the Sangría and place in the wine glass. Pour in your desired amount and enjoy. This drink is great for a nice sunny day. Make sure you store any remaining Sangría in your refrigerator until you are ready to enjoy. Typically your pitcher won't stay full for long.

# Woo Gal*

1 once of Soju

1 once of peach schnapps

4 ounces of cranberry juice

Ice

1. Add ice to a tall glass and a cocktail shaker.

2. Add Soju and Schnapps to the cocktail shaker. Cover and shake for around 20 seconds.

3. Pour contents of contain shaker into the tall glass you filled with ice.

4. You can garnish with a piece of fresh fruit if you like. I like to keep this one simple. I also prefer to serve this drink in a plastic cup for nostalgic reasons!

\* The Origin story of the "Woo Gal" cocktail dates back to my time spent in Okinawa. Some friends and I held monthly BBQ's in the maintenance dorms, when I was stationed on Kadena Air Force Base. We all missed the BBQ's from home, so we decided that we would recreate that feeling in our dorm. It started off small, but shortly grew into an anticipated event. We started off with burgers and hot dogs, but we stepped our game up and started to make steaks, shrimp, ribs and a bunch of other tasty things. We also stepped our drink making game up. Most of the fellas drank beer or simple mix drinks. One of my buddies started to make drinks for the ladies that didn't like beer or normal mixed drinks. The "Woo Gal" was a drink of choice. This drink didn't taste like alcohol so it was a crowd favorite! At times we even got fancy and served this drink inside of hollowed out pineapples. The drink started off as a similar drink that uses Vodka, but I decided to use Soju because it mask the alcohol taste better. The Soju that we used was direct from South Korea. The thing about the Soju that we used to get back then was ,you never knew what you were getting! Some bottles were stronger than others. You could get 3 bottles of the same brand and some were really strong, while others were weak! The "Woo" in the name of this drink comes from the war chant that sang out from most of the woman that drank it, after they had a few drinks. The "Gal" in the name of the drink derived from the name one of my dorm mates used to call all of the women that frequented our parties. He would approach the ladies and say "You's a hot Gal"! The corny pick up line never worked but it added a bit of funny commentary. I know the name is corny, but rest assured the drink is delicious!

# Beer Cola

1 12 once can of Cola

1 12 once German Wheat Beer

( preferably Hefeweizen )

1 Chilled 16 Once Pilsner Glass

1. Pour contents of beer into the chilled pilsner glass at an angle. Pouring the beer at an angle will keep your beer from foaming up too much.

2. Pour about 4 ounces of the cola in the pilsner glass.

3. Top off with additional beer or cola to adjust to your taste buds.

Last time I went to the Hofbrauhaus (German restaurant), I ordered a beer cola with Hefeweizen. My waiter knew exactly what I was asking for when I placed my order!

# Energy Drink Splash

4 ounces of energy drink ( I use the flavor free kind)

1 ounce of Vodka ( Optional )

1 splash of Grenadine

1.  Place a few ice cubes in a small glass (rocks glass)

2.  Add at least 1 ounce of vodka over the ice.

3.  Pour energy drink in your glass.

4.  Add a few splashes of grenadine and give your drink a few stirs.

The first time I was introduced to energy drink, I was in Germany. I arrived to Germany during the time the United States was involved in a conflict in Kosovo(1999).  My unit was tasked with helping NATO during this conflict. My shop was on extended hours during the whole conflict. We worked 6 days on and had 1 day off. At first, most Airmen only went to work and back home. After a few weeks of only going to work, I was getting frustrated. I needed to go out and blow off some steam. I met up with a few of the guys I knew in the dorms and they took me out to a local disco-tech. I met a German woman when I was at the bar and she asked me why I looked so tired. I explained to her that I had worked a lot of hours and was very tired.  The German woman told me that she has a drink that would help me wake up. At this point, I was willing to try anything because I didn't want to kill everyones vibe.  I don't know what portions the club used but over the years I have figured out my own portions. This drink is also my go to drink when I go out with friends and I don't want to drink alcohol. All I do is eliminate the vodka and folks think that I am drinking alcohol and don't harass me about not drinking with them.

# Cognac* & Pineapple

3 ounces of pineapple juice

1 ounce of cognac (Hennessy preferably)

1 handful of ice

...................................................................

1. Place ice cubes in a small whiskey glass. If you want to get fancy you can freeze some pineapple juice in an ice tray in advance if you know you are going to be making this. I think the pineapple ice cubes adds a good touch.

2. Pour cognac and pineapple juice over ice, stir gently and enjoy.

Maintenance dormitory parking lot, Kadena Air Base 1997

* I have a strong love for Hennessy (cognac)! Growing up I listened to a lot of hip hop. Most East Coast artist glorified Hennessy. One of my favorite groups (Mobb Deep) used Hennessy in many of their lyrics. On My 20th Birthday( I was in Japan and that was the legal drinking age) all my dorm buddies chipped in and bought me a bottle, so I could try it. I immediately grabbed my skateboard and did a victory lap in the dorm parking lot ! Every since my first experience with Hennessy, it has been one of my main go to drinks!

# Yummy Bears

1 large Bag of normal sized gummy bears

Vodka

1.  Pour gummy bears into an airtight container, making sure you leave enough room for the bears to expand.

2.  Pour enough vodka over the gummy bears to ensure that they are fully covered.

3.  Place your lid on the container and place in a cool dry place for at least 6 hours. I like to let them sit 6 hours and then place them in the fridge to firm up a bit.

4.  Yummy Bears are best when enjoyed within a reasonable time frame. They can become a little soggy if they are left sitting too long.

5.  If you want, you can use the liquid that is left behind from the yummy bears to make other cocktails.

6.  These bears pack a punch, so please enjoy responsibly!

Anything could happen during a Florida vs Georgia football tailgate. Yummy Bears were enjoyed by all in our group the day of these pictures . I wore a mask because it was during Halloween this particular year. I was probably telling my friend a joke and running away. I wonder what was so funny?

# Coffeeade ☕ + 🍋

Cold Brew Coffee

Lemonade

Ice

.............................................................

1.  Fill a cocktail shaker halfway with ice. Fill a glass halfway with ice.

2.  Fill cocktail shaker with a 50/50 mixture of Cold Brew coffee & Lemonade.

3.  Cover and vigorously shake cocktail shaker for 10-15 seconds.

4.  Pour mixture into glass and enjoy!

When I became a recruiter and moved to Jacksonville I found a new love for coffee. I drank coffee before moving to Jacksonville but the long hours and stress of being a recruiter and a recruiting supervisor made me really appreciate coffee on a different level. Recruiting offered me a lot of freedom on where I could work. When I became a recruiting supervisor I was given a wifi card that gave me the ultimate freedom to work where ever I wanted without having to use public wifi. I started to embrace the local coffee scene in Jacksonville. Bold Bean Coffee is by far my favorite place to get coffee in North Florida. The baristas always welcomed me and made me feel at home. They also pushed me to really enjoy coffee in its rare form. Before I started going to Bold Bean, I was never really adventurous when it came to coffee. I would only order a cappuccino every time I got coffee. One day a barista convinced me that I should try to taste a pour over coffee with out sugar or milk! I tried it and it wasn't bad. I eventually was able to cut all sugar or other additives from my coffee. My favorite way to drink coffee these day is in the form of a nitro cold brew. I came up with a nice coffee cocktail to enjoy on a warm day(or whenever).

# Chapter 2
# Sides

A good side dish will be a good compliment to any main. It is not the job of the side dish to be the headliner. A side dish should compliment and provide added support where the main falls short.

Most cooks will try to balance out each meal based on nutritional requirement or benefits. I feel that having a balanced diet is important but sometimes the logic can be thrown out the door when you are just cooking to make a good meal. I could personally care less how many starches or carbs are in a meal if all the flavors are on point.

I am always experimenting with new side dishes to accompany my main dishes. In this chapter, I will introduce you to some of my favorite side dishes! I often get asked to bring some of these dishes over to friends houses for cook-outs and get togethers.

Depending on how you execute, your side dishes will determine if they remain a side or become a main. Sometimes a few things can be added to a side dish that will help it stand alone as a main. I consider the recipes in this chapter to be sides but please use them as you see fit.

# SIDE DISHES

LEAK SOUP

HOT WINGS

BACON WRAPPED GREEN BEANS

CORNBREAD DRESSING

DRESSING WAFFLE

BAKED PASTA AND CHEESE

BUTTER NUT SQUASH SOUP

SWEVORY BUTTERNUT SQUASH

BUTTERNUT SQUASH RISOTTO

4 STAR MEATBALLS

WEDDING SOUP

BLACK BEANS

AVOCADO TOAST

WHITE BEAN DITALINI SOUP

LOBSTER QUESADILLAS

POTATO RÖSTI

When I first started dating my wife, I started having experiences that I always wanted to do but never had a reason to do so. I had always wanted to go to a 3 course meal on a date. Not some meal that you can get at a local family restaurant but the kind you see in movies with fancy tables and well dressed staff.

After about a year of dating I wanted to treat my then girlfriend to one of the meals I had dreamed of having. I was stationed in England at the time and I didn't really know what the best restaurant in our area was. Everyone in the area recommended that I take her to this place called Colleys Supper Rooms in a small town called Lechlade. Colleys was the type of place you see on TV shows about how old world England looks. When you walk in, a doorman escorts you and your party upstairs to a clock room where they take your coat and store in for you. When you are seated you are treated like a king and queen. Every detail was tended to! The table cloths felt as if they were freshly pressed the moment before you walked in the door. The decor was reminiscent of a scene out of an episode of Downton Abby.

The meal service was by far my favorite part of the whole experience. When it was time to select your entree, there was a long line of sue chefs that brought a real display of the meal selections to your table. It was a very surreal experience. The hardest part was selecting just one. Everything looked amazing! The one part of the meal that I remembered the most was a Leek and potato soup that was infused with truffle oil. At this time in my life I was about 25 years old and had never tasted a Leek, couldn't pick one out in a police line up, and didn't know what the hell a truffle was and why I wanted it's oil in a soup! With all that being said ,I was convinced to try it.

When I tell you that Leek soup was the best soup I had ever had in my life, I really mean it! At that point in the meal, I would have been satisfied to go home. Obviously I didn't leave but I was already impressed. My mission after I left that restaurant was to recreate that soup and introduce it to as many folks as possible. I am sure I will never know exactly how Colleys made their soup, but I feel I have a really good representation of what I had that day in Lechlade. I recently found out that Colleys shut their doors for good in 2018! It is a shame that they closed down because I had one of the best dinning experiences I have ever had there. I just hope other restauranteurs out there can emulate the type of experience that Colleys gave its patrons.

I plated the three bowls of my Leek Soup pictured above during a cooking competition I had against a good friend of mine. We were stationed in Germany at the time. Another friend of ours lived in a huge Farmhouse in a small village. The house had two kitchens. The competition was like a cooking show. We had a set amount of time for each segment. We had to have a starter, main and dessert. Our friend was hosting a baby shower that day. When we were done with each meal, our plates were taken to the guest. We had to describe what the dish was and what we used to make it. I ended up winning the competition, but everyone had a good time and that's what really mattered!

# Leek Soup

Making Leek soup is a bit of a process that takes some time and preparation. The finished product versus what the soup looks like cooking are way different. The above photo is was taken during the sautéing part of making the soup. The end result is totally worth all of the work it takes to prepare this dish.

# Leek Soup

3-4 Large Leeks

2 Large Yellow Onions

I bushel of green Onions

1/2 TBSP of minced garlic

6 slices chopped Bacon (optional)

Salt and Pepper

1-2 cartons of vegetable stock (chicken stock will work too)

1 cup of heavy cream( optional)

2 TBSP of Olive Oil or Butter

Truffle oil for serving (optional)

1. The first step to this recipe is one of the most important. You want to make sure you clean the leeks throughly. Leeks can be hard to clean because they have many layers. You will need to wash the surface area and then you will need to rewash after you cut your leeks. The leeks need to be sliced into 1/4 -1/2 inch slices. When I cut mine I discard the tough hard pieces near the top of the leaf and the root. Once you have sliced all leeks, you will need to separate each sliced piece. The sliced pieces will look like rings once they are separated. It is very essential to separate the slices because dirt somehow finds a way to get trapped inside the rings. The last thing you want is to see dirt in your pan when you are cooking your meal! The best way I have found to clean the leeks are to place them in a clean sink filled with warm water. I normally double or triple wash all of my leek pieces to ensure all the dirt is gone. Once you have completed this step drain all of the water from the leeks and set them aside.

2. Dice yellow onions, chop green onions, mince garlic, and chop bacon into small chunks.

3. Place olive oil or butter in a dutch oven or large pot. Add bacon and let it cook until if is almost crispy. Add garlic, onions and leeks to the pot and sauté. You want to cook all ingredients until they are almost translucent. You should add in your salt and pepper while your ingredients are sautéing. Remember that you also have bacon in your pot, so you will have to adjust your seasoning based on how salty your bacon is. You need to make sure that you occasionally stir your ingredients to make sure that they are not sticking or burning.

4. Pour in your cartons of vegetable stock. The stock should deglaze your pot and keep any flavor that is inside. You will need to adjust the amount of your stock depending on how thick you like your soup. I normally add about two cartons. You will need to cook your soup at a low simmer for about 15 -20 minutes.

5. If you want a thick soup you can leave it as it is. To make your soup smooth you will need to remove it from the heat and use an immersion blender to smooth your soup out. Once your soup is at your desired consistency, stir in the heavy cream. The soup is best if served immediately. Top off the bowl of soup with about a teaspoon of truffle oil.

When I was stationed in England, I got homesick for some good old American style hot wings. It's weird what you miss when you are out of the country. You can get hot wings in England but it just isn't the same as the ones you can get in America. Everyone has their favorite place to go to get wings in the states but I missed the ones I use to get at Hooters. Some of my friends didn't like the wings from Hooters but to me they are my go to if I want to watch a game and get some wings.

My frustration made me go in my kitchen to develop my recipe for my own wings, inspired by the ones I used to get at Hooters. It took me a few times to come up with a recipe that I felt was worthy to serve my friends! The day I decided to introduce my creation to my friends, there was a party going on at a friends house. I told my friend that I would provide wings for the whole party. With this knowledge, he didn't plan on buying any other meat to supply to everyone that was coming through. Once I found out that I was going to be the sole provider of protein at the party, I got a little anxious. Even though I was anxious, I was also excited. I am one of those type of people that do my best work under pressure.

I decided to up the ante and make jumbo buffalo style shrimp as well. No one knew I was coming through with these! I had planned on making the wings and shrimp at my house and just showing up ,but once I found out how many folks were coming through,I knew that all food needed to be made on site!

The pressure was on! Most of my friends that I surround myself with are not the types to bite their tongue. Most of them are very sarcastic and will tell it to you like it is. I love that about my friends but I wasn't trying to hear any negative reviews about my food! Hungry and bad food don't mix! If you are ever going to host a dinner party make sure you have tested your recipe before you invite your people over. There is nothing like showing up some where hungry, only to be served bad food! That's the quickest way to lose future attendees at your parties.

My wings and shrimp came out wonderful and everyone at the party was mad that I didn't bring more. I was presently surprised! I think I might have only had one hot wing and a couple of shrimp but I was just happy that people enjoyed my food. Some of my friends even said that they preferred my wings over ones they could buy at restaurants! I believe this is one of the best compliments a home cook could ever get. I hope you enjoy my hot wing recipe as much as I do.

# Hot Wings

1-2 pounds of chicken wings (Brined)

2 large Eggs

2 cups of milk

3 cups of all purpose flour

2 cups of butter milk (optional)

Basic rub ( any meat rub that you like for chicken)

1 bottle of hot sauce ( preferably Franks Red Hot )

Half a stick of butter

Salt

Pepper

Paprika

Vegetable or peanut oil

1. You should plan in advance if you want these wings to come out good. I put that you should used brined chicken if at all possible. Please see the page following this recipe for details on how to properly brine your chicken.

2. Rinse brine off of your chicken in cool water. Place cleaned chicken in a bowl or container and cover with buttermilk. Place container in the refrigerator for at least 2 hours.

3. Remove chicken from the refrigerator and rinse with cool water. Cover each piece of chicken with my rub recipe (or any rub) for maximum flavor.

4. Beat eggs in a large bowl and add 2 cups of milk. The milk wash that you are making will help the flour stick to your chicken better.

5. Use at least 3 cups of all purpose flour. You can use a large bowl or put your flour in a large brown paper bag. If you use the brown bag method make sure you watch for holes or use a double bag to prevent the chicken puncturing through. I like to season my flour and my chicken but it is totally up to you if you want to season both. If you brine your chicken it won't need as much seasoning but like I said it is all up to personal preference.

6. Pre heat oil to reach a temperature of 350 degrees F. I use a deep fryer because it keeps the temperature constant but you can also use a cast iron skillet or dutch oven for best results. The cast iron helps keep the temperature consistent. If you don't have a deep fryer, it might be a good idea to invest in a good thermometer. One of the keys to making good fried chicken is consistent oil temperature.

7. Place chicken pieces in bowl that contains your eggs and milk. You only need to place the chicken in long enough to place a light coating of the liquid on the chicken.

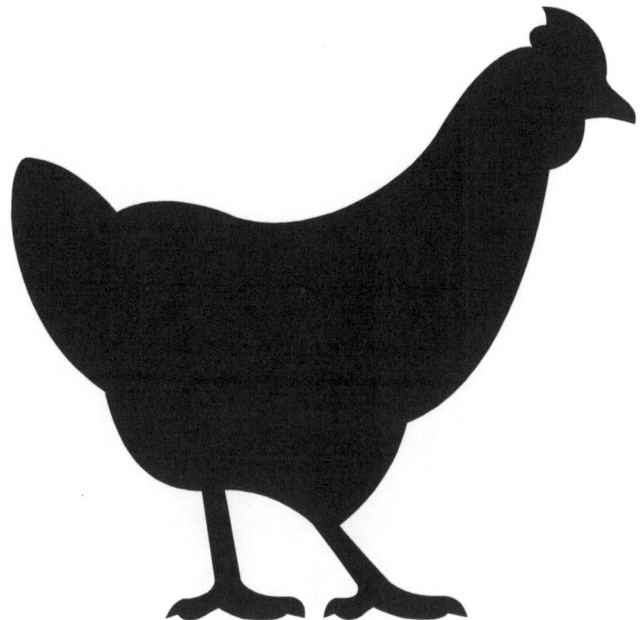

8. Put chicken in your bag or bowl that you filled with flour. Make sure chicken is completely coated with flour. Ensure to check for skin flaps that might be hiding an un flowered part of each piece of chicken.

9. Place chicken into frying oil. Be sure not to overfill your pan or fryer. The chicken should not be crowded. If you crowd the chicken, the flour from one piece will stick to another piece and it will make your chicken cook unevenly. Once your chicken is finished and done to your preferred crispness, remove from the frying pan and place on a metal rack to help drain some of the oil from the chicken.

10. While your chicken is frying, you should start working on your sauce. Place butter, hot sauce, pepper, salt, and paprika in small sauce pan. Bring sauce to a slow simmer making sure to stir in all of your ingredients. You want to make sure all of the butter is melted down and spices are well blended before you remove your sauce from the stove.

11. Now that all of your chicken is done and your sauce has had a few minutes to chill, you need to find a container or large pot with a lid that you can use to combine your chicken and sauce. Place chicken and sauce in your container/pot of choice. Cover the pot and shake/toss the wings in your sauce until the chicken is completely covered.

12. I know this recipe is for wings but I have used the sauce to cover fried shrimp as well. I am convinced that this recipe will be one of your go to recipes!

# Chicken Brine

I like to use Chicken brine when I fry or bake chicken. The brine acts as a wet marinade that will help penetrate the fibers of the chicken. I like to brine the chicken the morning of the day I'm cooking the chicken.  8-10 hours is a good amount of time to brine chicken.  Make sure that you don't let your chicken stay in the brine mixture longer than 24 hours.

| Ingredient | | Amount |
|---|---|---|
| Water | 4 | Cups |
| Kosher Salt | 4 | TBSP |
| Juniper Berries | 1 | TBSP |
| Crushed garlic | 4 | Cloves |
| Black pepper corns | 1 | TBSP |
| Honey | 3 | TBSP |

1.Empty all contents into a large pot and bring to a slow boil. Make sure that your stir the contents while the pot is on the stove. Allow the brine to cool to room temperature.

2.Place chicken in a sealable container. Pour cooled brine over pieces of chicken. Ensure that the chicken is submerged in the brine.

3. Put container in the refrigerator for 8-10 hours.

To prepare for cooking: Remove the chicken from the brine mixture and rinse with cool water.  Pat all excess water dry with a cloth before you use in any recipe.

# Bacon-N-Greens
### (BACON WRAPPED GREEN BEANS)

One bag of fresh green beans (1-2 Pounds)

1/2 pound of thin sliced bacon

Sea Salt

Fresh Cracked Black Pepper

Smoked Paprika

1. The first thing you need to do is prepare your green beans for consumption. Wash all of the green beans and snap the stems and ends on each green bean. This step can be time consuming but it is a must if you want the this side to turn out properly.

2. Fill a large pot with water and bring to a rolling boil. While your water is heating up fill a large bowl with ice water.  Add some sea salt to your water and place your green beans in to blanch them. Once your green beans are ready(their color should change and they will become more pliable) immediately pull them from the water and place in the ice bath that you prepared.

3. Preheat your oven to 375 degrees F. Divide your green beans into equal piles. You should be able to make 8-10 bundles from a normal 1-2 pound bag of green beans.  Wrap each pile with a piece of your bacon.

4. Arrange your wrapped green bean bundles on a baking pan evenly spaced. Season your bundles with sea salt, pepper, and paprika.

5. Place your pan in a preheated oven and cook until your bacon is done to your liking. Baking times will vary depending on the type oven you use, so be sure to monitor closely.

6. Remove from baking pan and place on cooling rack to help remove excess grease. For best results, serve hot.

# CORNBREAD DRESSING

AS LONG AS I CAN REMEMBER, MY FAMILY HAS BEEN EATING CORNBREAD DRESSING OR "DRESSING" FOR SHORT! I REMEMBER WATCHING COMMERCIALS AS A KID THAT WOULD ADVERTISE A CERTAIN BRAND OF STUFFING THAT YOU CAN MAKE ON YOUR STOVE TOP. I USE TO LOOK AT THE COMMERCIALS AND WANT TO TASTE THE STORE BOUGHT VERSION OF WHAT MY MOTHER AND GRANDMOTHERS ALWAYS MADE FROM SCRATCH. I USE TO FEEL LIKE I WAS MISSING SOMETHING BY NOT HAVING THE STUFF THAT WAS BEING CELEBRATED ON THE TV. THE FAMILIES IN THOSE COMMERCIALS USE TO MAKE ME JEALOUS BECAUSE I COULD NOT HAVE ANY. LITTLE DID I KNOW THAT I WAS EATING THE SUPERIOR PRODUCT IN MY HOME THE WHOLE TIME. I NEVER ASKED HOW MY MOM OR GRANDMOTHERS MADE THEIR DRESSING. I WAS JUST HAPPY TO BE ABLE TO EAT IT WHEN IT WAS DONE.

AFTER I JOINED THE MILITARY, I REALIZED THAT NOT ALL PEOPLE'S PARENTS AND GRANDPARENTS WERE ON THE SAME LEVEL AS MOST SOUTHERN MOMS AND GRANDMA'S ARE. I STARTED TO ASK SOME OF MY FRIENDS WHEN I WAS AWAY AT TECHNICAL TRAINING SCHOOL WHAT THEIR FAVORITE MEAL WAS DURING THE HOLIDAYS. WE WOULD OFTEN TALK ABOUT WHAT WE MISSED FROM HOME(ESPECIALLY AROUND THE HOLIDAYS). I ALWAYS SAID, DRESSING WAS THE THING I MISSED THE MOST! I MISSED MY FAMILY BUT I STARTED TO REALLY MISS SOME OF THE MEALS AND DISHES THAT I ONCE TOOK FOR GRANTED. WHEN I WAS AT MY FIRST BASE, I WENT INTO THE COMMISSARY ON BASE AND BOUGHT SOME OF THAT STUFFING THAT YOU CAN MAKE ON YOUR STOVE. TO SAY I WAS DISAPPOINTED AT HOW THE STUFFING CAME OUT WOULD BE A HUGE UNDERSTATEMENT! AT FIRST BITE, I WAS LIKE 'WHAT IS THIS?" GROSS! SOME PEOPLE LOVE THIS STUFF, BUT WHEN YOU GROW UP EATING SOUTHERN STYLE DRESSING, THIS STUFFING THAT IS MADE FROM THE BOX WILL NEVER TRULY SATISFY YOUR CRAVING. IT WAS AT THIS MOMENT THAT I KNEW I NEEDED TO PRESS MY MOM TO GET THE SECRETS TO HER DRESSING. HER RECIPE HAS EVOLVED OVER THE YEARS BUT I THINK I HAVE A GOOD GRASP ON HOW SHE USE TO MAKE IT. THE RECIPE THAT IS IN THIS BOOK MAY SEEM LIKE A LITTLE OVER KILL FOR A SIDE DISH, BUT I FEEL LIKE IT IS WORTH IT.

I FEEL THAT COOKING IS BORN FROM PASSION. CHEFS AND HOME COOKS ALIKE ARE DEDICATED TO PUTTING THEIR HEARTS AND MINDS INTO MAKING THE BEST DISH THAT THEY CAN IN ORDER TO SATISFY THE PEOPLE THAT ARE GOING TO CONSUME THE DISH/MEAL. I TYPICALLY ONLY MAKE DRESSING AROUND THE HOLIDAYS BECAUSE IT IS RATHER TIME CONSUMING AND I ALSO RELY HEAVY ON A TURKEY FOR SOME KEY COMPONENTS. I AM ALSO NORMALLY NOT WORKING AS MUCH AROUND THE HOLIDAYS AND HAVE MORE TIME TO MAKE THIS DISH WITHOUT FEELING RUSHED. I HOPE YOU ENJOY THE RECIPE AND KNOW MANY YEARS OF TRIAL AND ERROR HAVE GONE INTO THIS RECIPE. MODIFY AS YOU SEE FIT FOR YOUR TASTE BUDS.

# SOUTHERN STYLE DRESSING

1 PAN CORNBREAD , CRUMBLED  (MADE IN ACCORDANCE WITH CORN MEAL MIX)

1 CAN OF CREAM OF CELERY SOUP

1 CAN OF CREAM OF CHICKEN SOUP

2-3 BUNCHES OF GREEN ONIONS (CHOPPED)

3 CELERY RIBS, CHOPPED

2 MEDIUM ONIONS DICED

3 CUPS OF BREAD CRUMBS OF YOUR CHOICE

TURKEY STOCK (32 OUNCE)

2 LARGE EGGS, LIGHTLY BEATEN

1 TSP DRIED SAGE

4 OUNCES FRESH TURKEY DRIPPINGS (OPTIONAL)

THIS IS WHAT MY DRESSING NORMALLY LOOKS LIKE WHEN I PUT IT IN THE OVEN. I PREFER TO USE A CAST IRON SKILLET, BUT IT ISN'T NECESSARY.

1.    ADD 2-3 TABLESPOONS OF BUTTER TO A LARGE SKILLET. SAUTÉ CELERY, GREEN ONIONS, AND ONIONS. YOU CAN SUBSTITUTE BACON FAT FOR THE BUTTER IF YOU WANT TO ADD MORE FLAVOR.

2.    IN A LARGE BOWL, COMBINE CRUMBLED CORNBREAD, BREADCRUMBS, SAGE, CREAM OF CELERY SOUP, CREAM OF CHICKEN SOUP, EGGS, AND SAUTÉED VEGETABLES. WITH A LARGE SPOON BEGINS TO STIR ALL ITEMS TOGETHER. SLOWLY START TO ADD TURKEY STOCK INTO YOUR MIXTURE ABOUT A CUP AT A TIME. ADD TURKEY DRIPPINGS AT THIS TIME AS WELL. DEPENDING ON HOW ABSORBENT YOUR BREAD IS, WILL DETERMINE HOW MUCH STOCK YOU WILL NEED. YOU DON'T WANT YOUR MIXTURE TO BE RUNNY, BUT YOU DON'T WANT IT TO BE DRY EITHER. I LIKE MY DRESSING TO HAVE A NICE CRUSTY TOP AND A MOIST CENTER. THE MIXTURE SHOULD HAVE A NICE BOUNCE TO IT WHEN YOU SHAKE THE BOWL.

3.    POUR MIXTURE INTO A PRE-GREASED CASSEROLE OR SUITABLE BAKING DISH. I TYPICALLY USE A LARGE CAST IRON SKILLET  BUT ANY LARGE SIZE BAKING DISH WILL DO.

4.    BAKE IN A 350° F OVEN FOR ABOUT 30-40 MINUTES. THE TOP SHOULD BE GOLDEN BROWN AND SHOULD HAVE A SLIGHT CRUSTY FEEL/LOOK TO IT.

# Dressing Waffle

2 cups of leftover cornbread dressing

1 large egg

1/4 - 1/2 cup of water

Leftover turkey, gravy and cranberry sauce

Preheated waffle iron( Belgian Style works the best)

1.Break dressing into small chunks in a medium to large mixing bowl.

2. Add water a little at a time and begin to mix dressing with a large spoon. Depending on how dense your dressing is, you might need a little more water than the recipes calls for. You want the dressing mix to be pourable but not runny.

3. Slightly beat egg and mix into your dressing. I like to use an egg to help keep the dressing together once it hits the waffle iron. Make sure you have a smooth but not runny texture. If need be, add water a little at a time until you get a good texture.

4. Spray your preheated waffle iron with cooking spray. I set the temp to medium when I make mine. Your dressing is already cooked, so at this point you are just cooking the egg and putting a nice crust on it.

5. While your waffle is cooking, reheat some of your left over turkey and gravy. When the waffle is done cooking, gently remove it from your waffle iron and garnish with your turkey and gravy. I like to put cranberry sauce on mine as well.

This dish is a great way to enjoy left overs the day after Thanksgiving if you or your family cook traditional meals around that time of year. If you like this dish, you should try to cook dressing more often, so you can enjoy it more (like I do)!

# Baked Pasta and Cheese

1 package of Pasta (16 ounce)

1 can of condensed milk

1 tbsp of sea salt

2 eggs

2 tsp of fresh black pepper

1 tsp of powdered mustard

1 tbsp sugar

2  8 ounce packages of cheese of your choice(I normally use extra sharp cheddar and colby jack)

2-3 tbsp of non-salted butter

1.    Empty can of condensed milk into a medium size mixing bowl. Add 2 eggs, pepper, salt ,sugar and powdered mustard and whisk until everything is mixed thoroughly. Set aside for now.

2.    Shred both blocks of cheese making sure to reserve the last quarter of each block . Chop the remaining cheese into small chunks. I like to distribute these small blocks throughout the pasta before I bake it.

3.    Prepare pasta in accordance with instructions on pasta packaging. I always add sea salt and olive oil to the water I am boiling my pasta in. This is totally optional but you might sacrifice some flavor if you skip this step.  Preheat your oven to 350 degrees.

4.    Drain water from pasta. It is easier if you leave the pasta in your pot. Make sure you get all of the water out of the pasta before you proceed. Mix butter and shredded cheese until the cheese is fully melted.

5.    Transfer pasta into a buttered or sprayed 13x9 deep oven dish. Pour milk mixture into pasta and mix. Put the chucks of cheese in and make sure they are mixed in evenly. If you want more cheese you can opt to top your pasta with more shredded cheese.

6.    Bake pasta in the oven until you have a nice golden brown crust on top. The time will vary depending on how fast your oven cooks. Make sure you monitor your pasta but normally it should take less than 30 minutes.

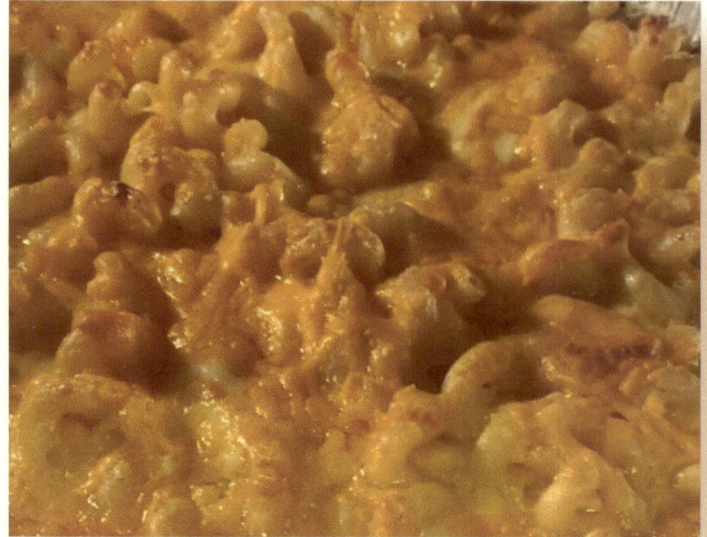

The reason why I call this "pasta and cheese" is because I like to use more than just macaroni. I get irritated when someone calls a dish macaroni and cheese and it has a different type of pasta. I'm not knocking macaroni but there are a lot of great pasta's that pair well with a cheese sauce. Some of the pasta's I like to use instead of macaroni include but are not limited to Cellentani, Fusilli Bucati Corti, Pipette Rigate, Campanelle, and Sendanini Rigati. I like to use pasta that has a an area for the cheese sauce to ooze into while cooking. If you have never made baked pasta and cheese before, I would recommend that you start with a classic elbow macaroni and then evolve from there.

# Butternut Squash Soup

**Butternut Squash (I use my swevoury squash on next page)**
**32 ounces of vegetable stock**
**Immersion hand blender or blender**
**1 tbsp of olive oil**
**Small container of heavy cream (optional)**
**Salt and pepper to taste**

1. Add olive oil to a large pot. Place all of the contents from the pre cooked butternut squash in the pot. Make sure you cook the squash until it starts to sizzle.
2. Add stock to your pot and deglaze any bits of squash that may have stuck to the sides or bottom of the pot.
3. Bring mixture to a low simmer. I like to let the mixture simmer for about 10 minutes.
4. Remove the pot from the heat and blend with a hand immersion blender. I like to use the hand blender because it's less messy than trying to transfer the mixture to a blender. If you don't have a hand blender, you need to carefully transfer all of the mixture into a blender. If you use a blender, you need to make sure you don't fill the blender up. The heat from the mixture will expand when it's blended, hence the reason I like to use a hand blender.
5. I like my soup to be smooth, so I blend it pretty well. If you like your soup chunky, make sure you give the blender a slight pulse until you reach the desired consistency.
6. Taste the soup to see if you need to add any salt or pepper.
7. If you like creamy soup, you should add the heavy cream in at this point and give it a good stir.
8. I like to serve this soup as a side dish, but if you add some bread it can definitely stand on its own.

# Swevoury* Butternut Squash

1 Large Butternut Squash

Olive oil

Salt & Pepper

Bacon( Optional )

1/2 Tsp Cinnamon

2 TBSP Brown Sugar

1.   Peel the squash and cut off the stem at the top. Be aware that the squash will become very slippery once you start to peel it.

2.   Once the squash has been peeled, you will need to cut it in half. The bottom of the squash houses all of its seeds. You need to use a spoon to scoop out all of the seeds. Give both sides a quick wash. Cut your squash into 1 inch cubes. The cuts don't have to be perfect but they should be as close to equal in size to ensure they cook at the same speed.

3.   Preheat oven to 350 degrees F. Combine cinnamon and brown sugar and set aside.

4.   Cut bacon into small slices. The amount that you use is totally up to you but make sure you don't over crowd your baking sheet.

5.   Arrange cubed squash and bacon on a large baking sheet. Drizzle with olive oil and season with salt and pepper to taste.

6.   Place baking sheet in oven and cook for about 20 minutes. A good way to tell when your squash is done is to look at how fast the bacon is cooking.  The squash should be fork tender when it is done. About 5-10 minutes before you pull from the oven sprinkle with cinnamon and brown sugar.

7.   Serve immediately or save for use with other dishes.

* Swevoury (swē-və-rē) This is the word that I like to use to describe a dish that is both sweet and savory. I've never heard anyone else use this word but I think it definitely has its place in the culinarily spectrum! Remember where you read about it first!

# Butternut Squash Risotto

**1 cup of arborio rice**

**2 shallots diced small**

**4 cups of chicken or vegetable stock**

**2-4 cups of roasted butternut squash(see previous page)**

**Sea salt and fresh black pepper**

**2 tablespoons Olive oil**

**1/2 cup of white wine**

**1/2 cup of freshly grated parmesan cheese**

1. Place chicken stock in a medium size sauce pan and bring to a slow simmer. Keep warm.

2. Heat oil in a large skillet over medium heat. Add diced shallots and cook until they start to turn golden brown. Season with sea salt and pepper to taste. Add rice and stir around pan until it is completely coved with oil. Level rice out making sure all pieces are in contact with the skillet surface.

3. Let rice cook until it starts to turn a slight brown color. It should smell like you are lightly toasting the rice. Pour white wine over rice and stir until all the liquid has cooked off.

4. Add a ladleful at a time (about 1/2 cup) of chicken stock. Stir until all of the chicken stock has been absorbed by the rice. Repeat this process until all of your stock is gone. This typically takes about 20-25 minutes.

5. Add roasted butternut squash and stir with rice until it is fully integrated. Season with salt and pepper again if needed.

6. Sprinkle freshly grated parmesan cheese over your dish. This dish is best served fresh. Even though I have it down as a side dish, it is hearty enough to be a one plate meal!

One of my Aunts is a vegetarian. I took this photo when I visited her a few years ago. I wanted to make a meal for her that was tasty and meat free. The only thing I had to omit was the bacon from the swevoury butternut squash.

# 4 Star Meatballs

★★★★

1 pound of sweet Italian sausage(buy uncased if you can)

1 pound of ground beef

1/2 cup chopped fresh basil

3/4 cup grated Parmigiana Cheese

2 Eggs

1/2 cup Italian bread crumbs

Salt

Pepper

Minced garlic

2 Tablespoons Olive oil

1. In a large bowl, combine all ingredients except the olive oil. Make sure that all ingredients are evenly mixed. I personally like to mix the ingredients with my hands. This step can get a little messy but when you mix with your hands you can feel the different textures as you combine your ingredients.

2. Grab enough of your mixture to create the desired meatball size you would like.  Once you have the desired amount of mixture in your hand , roll mixture until you form a ball. Place your completed meatball on a pan and repeat the process until all of your mixture is converted into meatballs. I typically use larger meatballs if I am going to make spaghetti or meatball subs.  If I am making Baked Ziti or soup, I tend to make smaller meatballs. The choice is yours.

3. Place olive oil in a large skillet over medium heat.

4. Place enough of your meatballs in the skillet to fill it but not over crowd it. If you are going to use your meatballs in a sauce or soup you can give them a good sear and pull them from the heat. Continue this process until you have seared all remaining meatballs. When you sear the meatballs they will still be raw in the middle but they will continue to cook if you put them in a sauce or soup. If you plan on the meatballs as a stand alone meal, you will need to make sure that you cook them all the way through.  I never make these as a stand alone meal. When I add the meatballs to another meal, I typically let them simmer in the sauce or soup for about thirty minutes.  I've noticed that when I finish the meatballs in my sauce or soup, the meatballs are more flavorful because they have time to absorb from the source that they finish cooking in.

# Wedding Soup

1 Large container of fresh spinach (or 2 cans of fresh cut spinach, drained)

10-15 baby carrots sliced

1 pound of sweet or spicy Italian sausage

1 can of Cannellini beans (drained)

1/2 - 3/4 cup of Acini de Pepe pasta

1 tsp garlic powder

1 tsp of Mediterranean seasoning

1 small block of parmigiana cheese

2 32 ounce containers of chicken stock

1. Brown Italian sausage in a large pot or dutch oven. Drain excess fat once sausage is cooked through.  Remove sausage from pot and return pot to stove over medium heat

2. Add sliced carrots to pot over medium heat. Cook carrots until they start to become tender but make sure you don't burn them.

3. Add chicken stock to the pot and bring to a slow rolling boil. Add in garlic powder, Mediterranean seasoning and cooked Italian sausage.

4. Shred small block of Parmigiana Cheese. Set shredded cheese aside. Place the rind of the parmigiana cheese inside the pot.

5. Reduce heat to a simmer and add in spinach. Cook uncovered until spinach is wilted and carrots are fork tender. Stir in Cannellini beans.

6. Add pasta to the soup mixture and cook for around 9 minutes.

7.  Add soup to a bowl and sprinkle with some of the shredded parmigiana cheese.

8. This soup is  best served fresh, but also reheats well. The pasta will absorb a lot of the stock base in this recipe. If you like your soup thinker, you need to use more of the pasta but not more than 3/4 of a cup.

When I went to Belize, I noticed that a lot of dishes were served with black beans and rice! Before going to Belize, I had only experienced black beans in Latin cuisine. I've made red beans and pinto beans before, but my travels to Belize inspired me to figure out how to make this dish on my own.

# Black Beans

**1 lbs of dry black beans**

**1 mediums size onion (chopped)**

**2-3 smoked ham hocks**

**salt and pepper to taste**

**garlic powder to taste**

**2-3 minced garlic cloves**

1. Soak beans in a large bowl with about 5-6 cups of water. Let beans sit in the bowl overnight. The beans will absorb the majority of the water.

2. Rinse beans with clean water. Add ham hocks, beans, onions, garlic, salt, pepper and garlic to a large slow cooker. I don't go crazy on the amount of salt that I use at this stage. When the hocks have time to cook, they will release some of their salt.

3. Cook on high for about 6 hours. I try not to bother the beans too much while they are cooking. I take the lid off the slow cooker every couple of hours to stir the beans.

4. Using a large spoon, search for any bones that might be in the beans. The hocks will break down to the point that all of the bones will come free. I like to make sure that all of the bones are gone before I serve the beans to anyone.

5. The black beans are great on their own, but they are better when mixed with freshly cooked rice!

# Avocado Toast

When I came back to the states after being stationed in Germany for a few years, I noticed a lot of things had changed. I went into a breakfast spot and avocado toast was on the menu. I had never heard of it before, so I gave it a try. I was surprised at how good it was but the $8 price tag was ridiculous! I think my version can hang with any one I ever bought.

# Avocado Toast

**1 ripe Avocado**

**Salt**

**Pepper**

**Garlic powder**

**Butter**

**2 slices of bread (multi grain works well)**

**2-3 eggs**

**1 slice of cheese**

**Everything bagel seasoning**

**1 small lime**

1. Slice open an avocado (the long way) down the middle. Remove the the pit from the center. Use a spoon to scoop out the contents into a bowl. Cut the lime in half. Squeeze the juice of one half of the lime into the bowl.

2. Use a large fork to mash the avocado. You want to make sure that you get the majority of the huge chunks out. Once the avocado is mixed to your desired consistency; season with salt, pepper and garlic powder. Go really easy on the garlic powder! You only need a small sprinkle. Set aside.

3. Add about a tablespoon of butter to a small frying pan over medium heat.

4. Crack your eggs into a small bowl and give them a slight stir to break the yolks. Pour the eggs into the pan and gently stir until the eggs are almost fully scrambled. Pull the pan from the heat and season the eggs with salt and pepper. Add the piece of cheese to the pan and stir until the cheese has melted into the eggs.

5. Put the bread into a toaster and toast to your desired doneness. Spread some butter onto your toast.

6. Spread an even amount of the avocado mixture onto each piece of the toast.

7. Place an even amount of the scrambled eggs onto each piece of the toast. Sprinkle a small amount of the everything bagel seasoning onto each piece of toast.

8. I like to serve this dish with fresh fruit. The toast is best served immediately.

I encourage you to change this recipe as you see fit to meet your specific taste buds. Every place I have ordered this dish puts a different spin on how they choose to make it. I really enjoy this recipe! The only thing I add to it from time to time is hot sauce. I hope you enjoy this dish as much as I do!

# White Bean Ditalini Soup

**4 star meatballs (See recipe 6 pages back)**

**1 15 ounce can of tomato sauce**

**1 15 ounce can of cannellili beans (drained)**

**1 large container of fresh spinach**

**2 large stalks of celery (chopped)**

**2 large carrots (peeled and chopped)**

**1 large Onion (peeled & diced into small chunks)**

**1 large zucchini (diced)**

**1 16 ounce box of Ditalini Pasta**

**1 32 ounce container of vegetable stock**

**Salt and pepper to taste**

**1 tsp Mediterranean seasoning**

**2 tsp of minced garlic**

**Fresh Parmigiana Reggiano cheese with rind**

**Olive oil**

1.  Add about 1 tbsp of olive oil to a large pot or dutch oven over medium heat. Sauté onions, celery, zucchini and carrots until they start to get soft. The onions should be slightly translucent. Add in minced garlic. Season with salt and pepper to taste.

2.  Pour in vegetable stock and deglaze the pot. Stir in tomato sauce and Mediterranean season. If sauce seems too thick, add about a 1/2 to 1 cup of water. Add in 4 star meatballs and rind from the Parmigiana Reggiano cheese. If your meatballs are not fully cooked, you will need to simmer this dish (covered ) for about 30 minutes.

3.  Once the meatballs are cooked; add spinach, beans and pasta to soup mixture and cook for about 10-12 minutes. The soup is done once the pasta is cooked.

4.  To serve: Pour into a bowls making sure each person gets a bit of everything. Top with freshly grated Parmigiana Reggiano cheese.

# Lobster Quesadillas

2 medium size lobster tails

1 large shallot (or two medium) diced

3-4 mini sweet peppers (gutted and sliced)

1/2 Tbsp Recado (optional but makes a difference)

Two large tortillas

2 tbsp Butter

Mexican blend cheese

Salt and pepper to taste

1.  Use a knife or kitchen shears to cut the shells of the lobster. tails. Remove lobster meat and cut into small chunks. Place cut lobster into small bowl and mix with Recado, salt, and pepper.

2.  Place butter into a medium size skillet over medium high heat. Add shallots and peppers when butter has heated up. Sauté until mixture is tender and has a good color. You want the shallots to have a nice golden brown color.

3.  Add Lobster to the skillet and stir all of the contents. Lobster cooks fast, so you want to make sure you remove it from the heat once it begins to turn white. You don't want to overcook your lobster, because it will become chewy.

4.  Heat another skillet up to medium high heat. Place a tortillas on the skillet and give a generous sprinkle of cheese. Spoon some of the lobster filling onto one half of the tortilla. Once the cheese has started to melt and the tortilla is starting to brown on the bottom side, flip so that both sides form a half moon shape. Once the cheese is holding everything together, you may need to flip the quesadilla so the other side can cook a little more. All you are doing at this stage is cooing the cheese, so the choice is yours how long you cook the quesadilla. I like mine soft, so I pull it off once the cheese has melted. Repeat this step with the second tortilla.

5.  To serve: cut tortilla into wedges similar to slices of pizza. I like to have a little sour cream and hot sauce with mine as well.

# Potato Rösti

**3-4 medium sized Potatoes (preferably high starch European ones)**

**Salt and pepper**

**Garlic powder**

**1- 2 tbsp of butter**

1. Boil potatoes until they are soft to the point that a kitchen knife will easily pass through them. Drain and place in the refrigerator overnight.

2. Peel the skin off of the potatoes and grate them with the large section of a cheese grater.

3. Squeeze all of the excess water that might be in the grated potatoes.

4. Season potatoes with salt, pepper and garlic powder to taste.

5. Heat a pan to medium high heat and place butter in it. Once the butter has melted, add a nice handful of the potato mixture in. Use a spatula to form the potatoes into the shape of a pancake.

6. Let the Rösti cook until it is golden brown on the bottom. Once the Rösti is to your desired color, place a plate on top of the Rösti to help flip it without breaking it.

7. Cook Rösti until it starts to brown on the other side. You should be able to make a few Rösti with the ingredients in this recipe. The amount you make is determined on how large the rösti you decide to make. I like to make mine about 6 x 6 inches.

8. Rösti are good on their own but I like to pair them with a meat dishes, such as Zürcher Geschnetzeltes.

# Street Snacks

When I used to go visit family in Chicago, I spent most of my days in the streets with the local kids. The area where I stayed was a poor neighborhood near the projects. Some people that have never lived in the South Side of Chicago have a lot of negative things to say about it. I won't say anything bad about the South Side of Chicago, because my experience there was one of love. Most of the people there were not well off, but they were good hearted. I learned a lot about being a real man from people I met on my numerous summer trips to Chicago.

Most of the kids in the hood didn't have a lot of money back in those days, but we were still able to eat snacks fairly cheap. Some streets in the area I was at had a snack shop that was set up in someone's home(we called our spot the "Candy Lady"). The Candy Lady had all types of snacks at cheap prices. She had a nice assortment of candy that cost a penny. Penny candy was a huge thing back in the 90's. The corner stores had penny candy, but most were kind of far from our block. The Candy Lady had everything we needed! You could get flavored ice pops(made in small styrofoam cups), chips, sodas, quarter waters, honey buns and plenty of other things.

I had my go-to snack that a few of the neighborhood kids put me on to. When the Candy Lady would get low on chips, she would only have the plain potato chips left. I wasn't a fan of the original potato chips. One day we were in the shop and I told my friend that I wanted chips but all that was left was the original ones! He told me, "just make um hot chips". I was like, "how do I make plain chips, hot chips"? He was like, "check this out"! He opened the bag and sprinkled

some hot sauce inside. He then closed the bag by gripping it tight around the opening. He stared me down while he gave the bag a nice shake. He looked me in the eyes and said, 'try these"! When I tried the chips, it was love at first bite! I couldn't believe a simple few dashes of hot sauce could transfer some lame chips into a delicacy! Ha-Ha, maybe not a delicacy.

Southside of Chicago, circa 1990

# Street Snacks (Hot Chips)

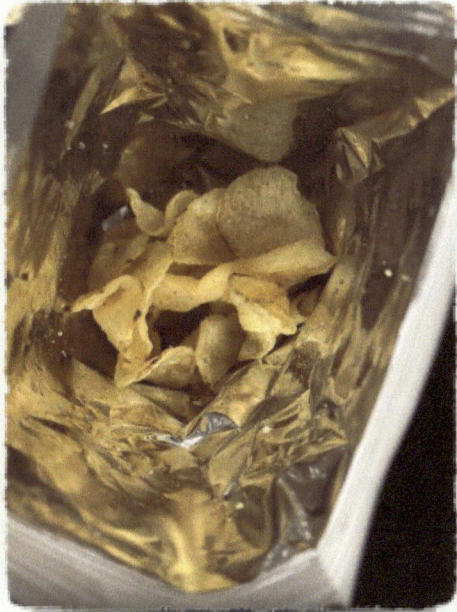

**Step 1**: Open the bag of plain potato chips.

**Step 2**: Add a few dashes of your favorite hot sauce to the bag. Don't add too much hot sauce, because it will make the chips soggy.

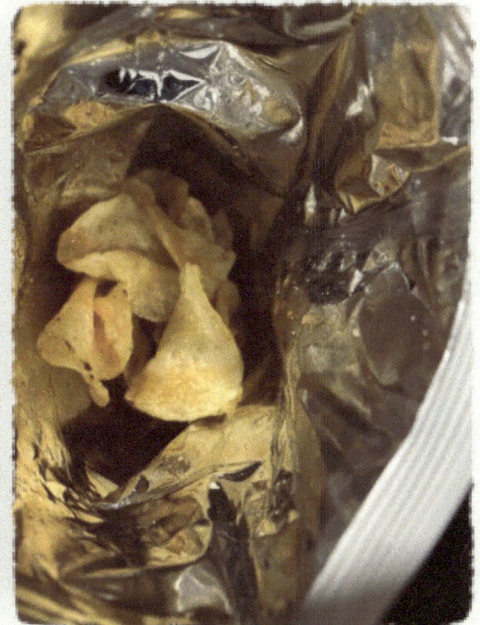

**Step 3**: Hold the bag of chips close at the opening and give a vigorous shake. Open and enjoy! Be careful because these chips are addicting.

# Spotlight: Belize

**A** few years ago one of my friends told me that him and his wife purchased a plot of land in Belize. They originally went to Belize on their honeymoon. While they were there, they posted some amazing pictures on social media detailing their trip. I was very intrigued about the idea of going to Belize one day.

The same friend came up with an idea of a group trip to Belize. My wife and I were down to go because we love to travel and we know we travel well with the group of people that went.

We traveled to Ambergris Caye. We chose this destination because it's a beautiful area and our friend said that there was going to be Lobster Festival during the time that we were going. Honestly, I was more excited about the local cuisine but I wasn't going to turn my nose up at a lobster fest either!

The island was nice but it was still a little rustic. We rented a huge house on the ocean and used gas golf carts to get around. The island has limited cars, so most of the traffic you see on the streets are golf carts. I've never been to a place like it!

I can't remember having a bad meal while we were there. I'm pretty sure everywhere we went our food was made to order. I remember trying to dissect the flavors of everything I ordered. I was in the process of writing this book, so I knew that I wanted to try to capture a feeling in a dish. All of the tortillas that we ate were fresh! There was a beach house being built next to the place where we were staying and the construction crew had fresh breakfast tacos delivered to them everyday. It didn't take our crew long to catch on and get in on the fresh taco action!

One day we all went to a restaurant on the beach and I ordered the specials of the day. Since the island was in Lobster Fest mode, the specials were lobster pie and lobster quesadillas. The lobster pie was decent but it didn't have anything on the lobster quesadilla's! I was instantly hooked! I knew at that point that I needed to figure out how to recreate this dish. Since lobster was in high supply, many different restaurants had their own version of lobster quesadillas. I think I ordered the dish from three different places. All of the restaurants cooked their quesadillas slightly different, but they were all delicious.

I picked up a few seasonings while we were in the Airport that are unique to Belizean cuisine. I felt that I had a better chance of capturing/recreating a dish if I had authentic spices. I like to try to grab regional spices and honey wherever I go. I grabbed some Recado spice paste and some seafood seasoning. The Recado paste has a unique taste to it. I'd never heard of it before my trip to Belize. I use some Recado in my lobster quesadilla recipe. I think my lobster quesadilla recipe comes pretty damn close to the ones I enjoyed in Belize. Whenever I want to take a mental and culinary trip back to Belize, I cook one of the dishes I enjoyed while I was there.

# Belize

# Spotlight: Romania

A few years ago, I was informed by a longtime friend that him and his family were going to get relocated to Romania. My wife and I were invited to go and visit them once they got settled in. My wife and I love to travel and we were 100% down to go visit them. We didn't have any expectations before going on our trip to Romania. We told our friends that we were more interested in hanging out with them in their city. We don't like people to make a big fuss when we come to town. We told them, all we really wanted to do is hang out and eat some good food!

Our friends lived in the capital city of Bucharest, so there was a lot of cool things to see and places to eat there. We were also lucky enough to travel by train to the city of Brasov. We stayed in a Guesthouse style hotel in the center of the city while in Brasov. It was such a cool little get away. The center of the city was decorated heavily for Christmas. We had a nice view of the city's Christmas market outside of our room.

One of my fondest memories of living in Europe was going to Christmas markets. Most of the bigger cities that I visited in Eastern Europe had Christmas markets during the the month of December. The markets are a one stop place for entertainment ,shopping ,food, festivities, and holiday spirit. I was thankful that we were fortunate enough to visit Romania in December. The Christmas markets in Brasov and Bucharest gave me a nostalgic feeling. I tie the nostalgic feeling to being in Europe in the winter.

The best way I can describe the vibe at a Christmas market to someone that hasn't been to one would be; State Fair/Farmers market/Folks festival. I hope that makes sense. Overall, they are cool places to hang out!

The people in Romania were very nice and welcoming. I felt that all of the people that we came in contact with treated us with respect. People seemed intrigued when a group of Americans walked in to a store or restaurant ,but I never felt threatened or disrespected.

My wife and I agreed that we would be down to travel back to Romania in the future. I felt like our experience was enhanced because our friends lived, and worked in the country. We probably wouldn't have had as much insight without our friends. I took a few pictures while we were there and included a few on the next couple of pages.

# Spotlight: Romania

Growing up in the south, I've eaten my fair share of ham hocks. When I walked around a Christmas market in Bucharest, I was looking for something that looked tasty that I probably wouldn't find in a restaurant. I came across a food stand that a bunch of locals seemed to be interested in. The smell coming from that stand was amazing! I asked the guy that was in charge what the best thing he had was. He pointed to the ham hock. He asked if I wanted a whole plate and I told him to serve me the dish how it is traditional served. The guy seemed to be very excited that I wanted to try his featured dish. I took the above photo right before my I got my to go box.

I didn't know what to expect, taste wise when I took my first bite of this ham hock. The fact that I was able to cut the hock with a plastic knife was a good sign. The taste that I experienced was one that I had never had before! It was the best damn ham hock I had ever had in my life! The cabbage that was served with the hock had a paprika flavored sauerkraut taste. I could also taste the juices that were present in the ham hock throughout the sauerkraut. The hock had a nice balance of flavor and spice. In my eyes this was culinary gold! It was the best dish I had while in Romania (that is saying a lot). After I devoured my plate, I went back to the stand and thanked the guy that suggested I get the dish. He had the biggest smile on his face when I told him how good it was! I was mad at myself later that night for not getting another portion to take back to my friends place!

# Spotlight: Romania

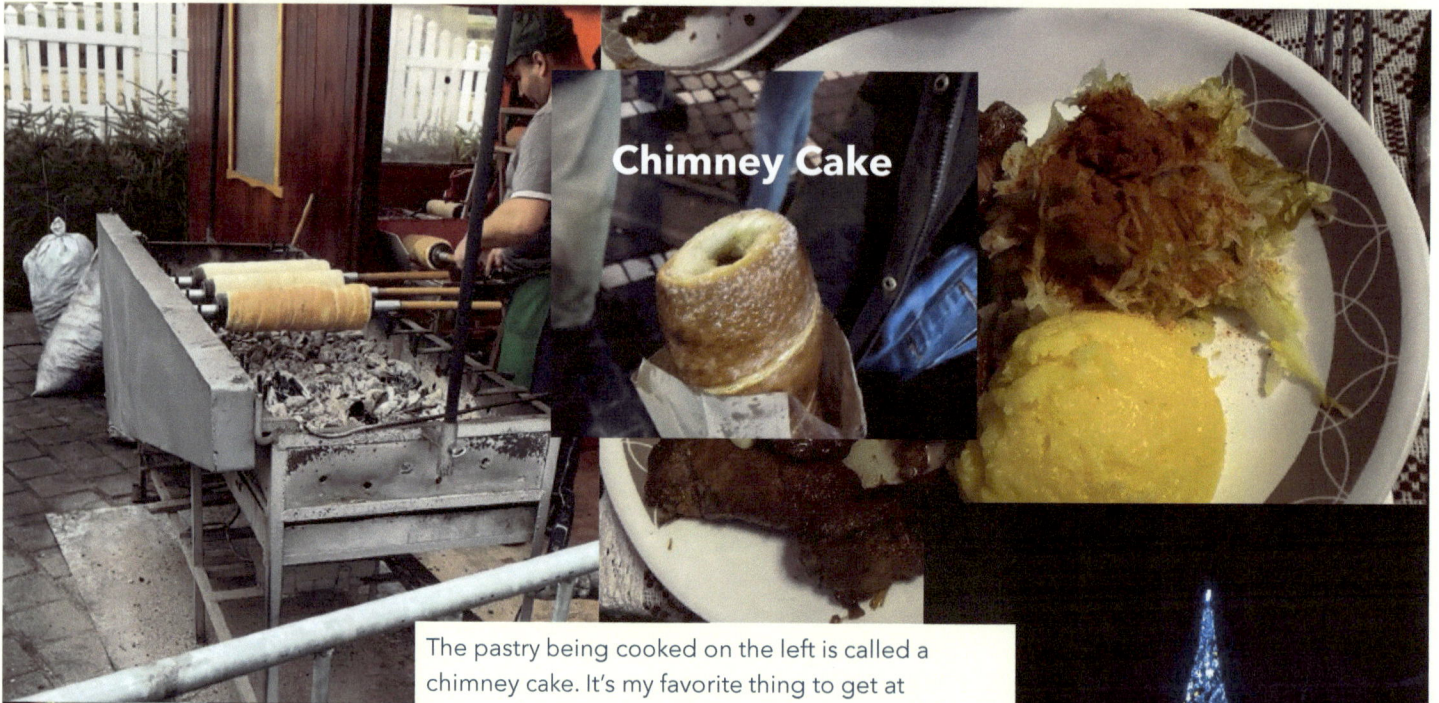

**Chimney Cake**

The pastry being cooked on the left is called a chimney cake. It's my favorite thing to get at European Christmas markets! When I lived in Germany, I could smell the chimney cakes as soon I stepped into a Christmas Market. The smell alone would put me in a good mood. After the pastry is finished cooking, it is normally dipped in cinnamon sugar or some other type of sweet mixture. Recently, I've seen some ice cream shops in the United States using chimney cakes as cones.

# Spotlight: Romania

Most of the pictures above are from Christmas Markets in Romania. The picture in the top right is from an eclair shop in Bucharest. My friend told me they were really good, so we went there and got a mixed box. I've had eclairs in France and other places that claim to be French restaurants. None of the eclairs I've had before were as good as the ones I had from this shop in Bucharest!

# Spotlight: Deutschland

# GERMANY

I can link a lot of my culinary exploration to the country of Germany! I spent a little over 5 years combined living in Germany. I was initially sent to Spangdahlem Air Force Base (AFB) right before reaching my 3 year anniversary of joining the Air Force. This was a very critical time for me in my military career. When I originally put in for the assignment, I was unsure if I even wanted to be in the military anymore. I initially only joined to get out of Georgia and to see a little bit of the world. I had only signed up for 4 years and I knew that I would soon have to decide if I would get out at my 4 year mark. I was banking on Germany to help me determine if I was going to reenlist.

When I arrived we were in the middle of a conflict with Kosovo. Half of my shop was deployed and I was immediately put on 12 hour shifts(6 days on with 1 day off). I wasn't convinced that I would want to stay in the Air Force based on my first couple of days in country. Most of my co workers were welcoming, and had a lot of great things to say about the local cuisine. When you are working all day and worried about your future, food can often provide a good amount of comfort. Germany didn't disappoint in helping me get over my slump. It was late spring time when I first arrived and the days were very long. I couldn't believe that it was still sunlight out at 8 and 9 o'clock at night. I had never been anywhere where I could still enjoy the day light that far into the night. Even after what equated to about a 14 hour workday (when you include getting ready and getting home), we still found a way to enjoy the rest of the daylight. We would find a spot to go eat some great food and knock back some nice German beers often.

It didn't take me long to start exploring all of the local restaurants and festivals. Germany help me decide that my time in the Military could not end at my 4 year mark. I had a 2 year assignment to Spangdahlem and the only way I was going to make it the whole 2 years was to either reenlist or extend my enlistment. It took me less than 4 months to decide to reenlist for another 4 years. In the 2 years that I was stationed at Spangdahlem, I was able to deploy to Spain & Croatia. I experienced my first trip to Las Vegas during this assignment on a temporary duty assignment as well. When people use to ask me what it was like being stationed overseas, the first thing I would talk about was all of the great food I was able to eat.

Spangdahlem AFB is located in the German Federal State of Rheinland-Pfalz. This region of Germany is geographically located around a lot of popular tourist destinations. We were close to Paris, Luxembourg City, Amsterdam, Cologne, Berne, Brussels, & Maastricht to name a few. With all of these cities at our disposal, it was hard at times to decide where we wanted to go spend our time. At times it was hard to believe that I was able to experience all of this culture at such a young age. Growing up, I only dreamed to be able to go to some of the same places I had seen in movies and eat the cuisine. Spangdahlem was my first European assignment but my last European assignment was also in Germany. My last overseas assignment was at Ramstein AFB. I was happy to be fortunate enough to experience Germany with my wife my second time around! Till this day, Germany still holds a special place in my heart. I still have friends in the country that I met through work or coaching. German food is definitely one of my favorite types of food in the world!

*The background image is from one of my going away plaques from Germany*

# Chapter 3
# Grilling and Chillin'

I can't think of a more relaxing way to cook then sitting around and grilling food. There is just something about smelling food cooking on a grill or smoker that puts me at ease. It took me a while to get to this state of mind!

I used to be intimidated by the concept of cooking on a grill. I feel that once you get a bbq grill going, you open yourself up for instant judgment! Some will be excited by the fact that you plan to cook something over live fire, some will hang around to see if you know what you are doing, some will try to micro manage everything you attempt to do, and some will hang around to see if they can learn something from you. Either way, you will be subjected to some type of judgement. The pressure of cooking on a grill can give most home cooks a level of anxiety that will make them not want to ever attempt to grill again. Don't let the pressure of grilling keep you from getting outside and creating some amazing BBQ!

I feel the skill of cooking with live fire is one that every home cook should learn!

Once you get in your grove and learn how to use your grill, grilling can be one of the most relaxing times you can have cooking. The "Chillin" in the chapter title comes from my mind state that I'm in when I'm on the grill. I get in a whole different vibe when I have meat on the grill and it's nice outside.

I put some of my favorite things to cook on the grill in this chapter. I hope that some of my favorites recipes can make their way into your next BBQ or get together. In any case, try not to be too intimidated about cooking on a grill. The best way to get better on the grill, is to put meat on the grill and learn!

# GRILLING AND CHILLIN'

BASIC BBQ DRY RUB

BRISKET

PORK BUTT

SMOKED RIBS

BALCONY STEAKS

SCHWENKBRATEN

BBQ CHICKEN

BAKED BEANS

YAKITORI

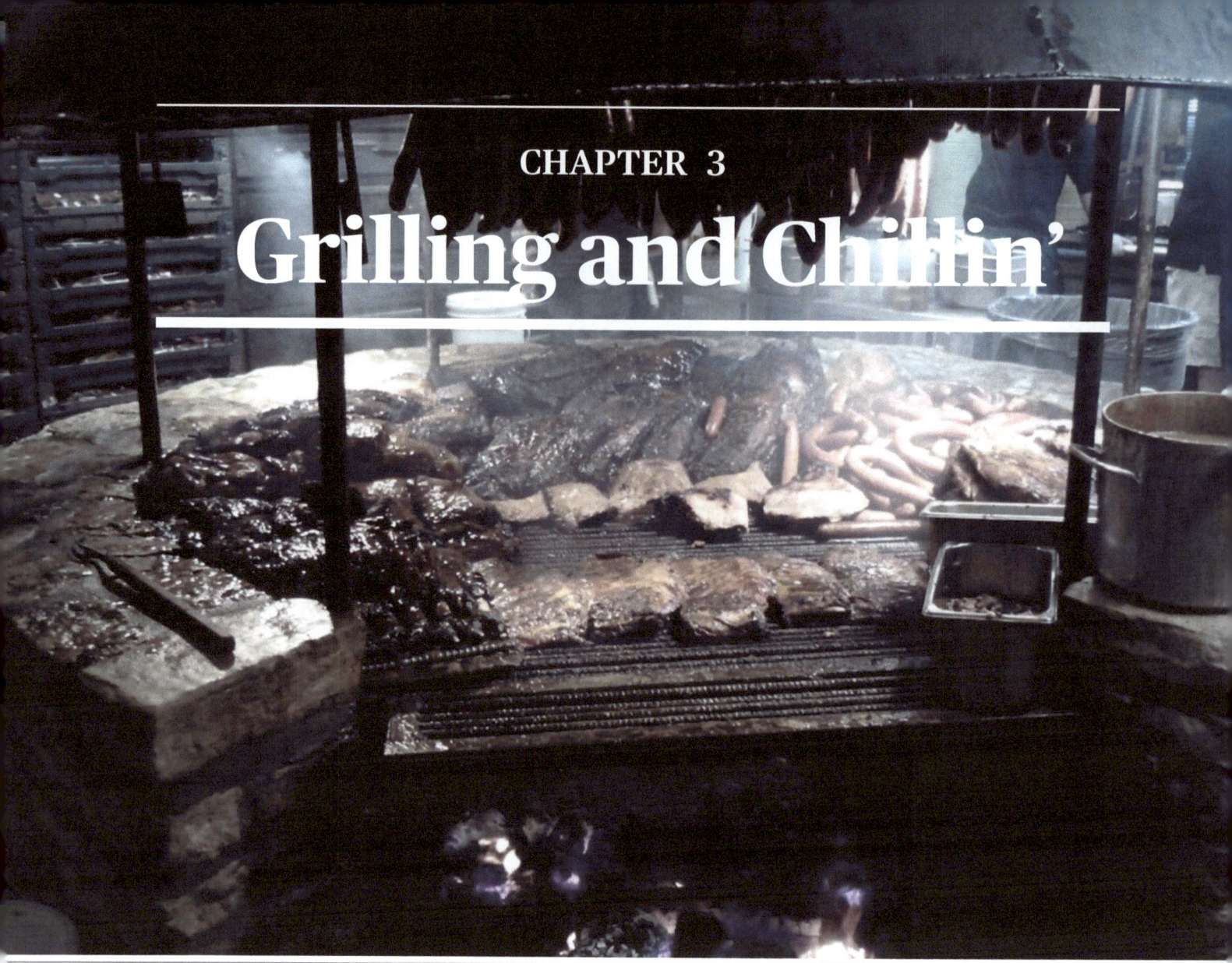

# Grilling and Chillin'

I took this photo at "The Salt Lick" in Driftwood, Texas. This is a great view but it fails to capture the magic of this establishment! Central Texas BBQ is some of the best BBQ in the world in my opinion!

# Basic BBQ Dry Rub

I like to use a dry rub on most things that I put on the grill. Sometimes wet marinades are good for certain dishes, but I like to stick with my dry rub for the majority of the things I make that aren't based on specific recipes. Below are the ingredients that I use for my basic dry rub. Sometimes I like to add other items to this base depending on what I'm cooking, but this is my trusted base rub. I prefer not to add sugar to my rub, because sugar sometimes causes flare ups when you are cooing with live fire. This rub doesn't only apply to BBQ. Use it with baking or frying meat as well.

| Ingredient | | Amount |
|---|---|---|
| Paprika | 2 | Tbsp |
| Salt | 1 | Tsp |
| Pepper | 1 | Tsp |
| Dry mustard | 1 | Tsp |
| Garlic Powder | 1 | Tsp |
| Onion Powder | 1 | Tsp |

Combine all of the ingredients and mix well. I use this rub as my basic rub. The amounts listed above should yield enough rub to cover one St. Louis style rack of ribs.

# Brisket

Brisket is my favorite meat to have whenever I go to a BBQ joint! I like the time and effort that goes into making brisket.

When lived in Texas as a kid, I never had enough money to buy brisket. I never even knew what it was as a child, if I'm being honest. Brisket has long been a heavy hitter in the Texas BBQ scene but it isn't a cheap cut of meat! I think I was in my 20's the first time I ever had brisket. I couldn't believe how good it was the first time I had it.

It wasn't long after I tasted brisket, that I wanted to try to cook it. I was blown away by the price when I went to check the grocery store! I couldn't justify spending anywhere between $50-100 dollars on one cut of meat. At that time I was a young Airmen and I could find a bunch of other things to spend that type of money on. Even today spending that much money on a cut of meat can be a big risk if you don't know how to properly cook it.

Needless to say, I didn't attempt to buy or make a brisket until many years later. I eventually took the risk and purchased my first brisket to make a few years ago. I was hella nervous! I had eaten brisket at many BBQ joints from many places at that point. I think I finally figured out what good brisket is supposed to taste like, in my opinion. I felt I was ready to attempt to cook one. I can't stress enough how much of a challenge this was for me. It took me almost 20 years or grilling to attempt to try to cook a brisket. I share that information because I want people to know that some meals you have to work up to. You should learn how to work a grill or a smoker before you attempt to cook a cut of meat like brisket. I

recommend that you try cooking cheaper cuts of meat before you try cooking a brisket. Obviously the choice is yours on what you decide to spend your money on. I think working with other cuts of meat help me understand smoke and fire better. I would hate for anyone to lose money by trying to figure out how to manage a fire with an expensive cut of meat on the grill.

As with most cooking, the more you cook something the better you get at it. Brisket is no different! I don't regret waiting to cook my first brisket. I enjoyed all the "taste test" that I did at all of those BBQ joints. I feel that I could have probably cooked a decent brisket a long time ago, had I not been so intimidated by it. I say all that to say this, don't be afraid to get your first brisket on the smoker!

BBQ boss

# Smoked Brisket

**1 9-12 lbs packer style brisket (trimmed)**

**1/2 cup of rub**

**Butcher or parchment paper (without wax backing)**

**Smoker or grill (with oak or cherry wood)**

**Plastic wrap**

**Instant read temperature probe**

**Water pan**

**Apple cider vinegar spray (optional)**

1. Open the brisket packaging and inspect it for excess fat and small thin pieces that will burn or dry out during cooking. Most briskets that come from the grocery store are decently trimmed but you still need to check. Rinse brisket with fresh water and pat dry.

2. Lay out brisket on a layer of plastic wrap big enough to cover the whole brisket. I normally have to overlap a few sheets.

3. Sprinkle the rub over all surfaces of the brisket. Make sure that you press the rub in with your hands. You want to make sure that the rub is generously applied to this huge cut of meat.

4. Wrap brisket in the plastic wrap and place in a plastic bag. The plastic bag will keep the brisket from dripping all over your refrigerator. Keep the brisket in the refrigerator overnight or about 8-10 hours.

5. Remove the brisket about 1-2 hours before you plan on smoking it. You want the brisket to come to room temperature before you place it on the smoker.

6. I like to cook the brisket at a steady 225 degrees F until it is done. Maintaining 225(or any temperature) on a smoker can or will be challenging. You need to make sure you monitor and adjust the heat as needed.

7. Insert temperature probe into the thickest part of the brisket. Be sure that the probe goes in straight and stays in the center of the meat.

8. Place brisket on the smoker fat side down in the coolest part of the smoker. Place a small pan of water on the other part of the grill. The water will help keep moisture while the brisket is cooking.

9. Check on brisket every few hours. If the brisket looks like it is drying out, give it a light spray of the apple cider vinegar.

10. When the brisket reaches an internal temp around 160 degrees, pull from the smoker and wrap with butcher or parchment paper. Place brisket back on the smoker and continue to cook until it reaches a temp of around 200-205 degrees. At this point your brisket will be very flexible.

11. Remove brisket from the smoker and leave it wrapped until you are ready to slice and serve. When you slice the brisket, you need to make sure you slice it against the grain of the meat.

12. I like to take the scraps or off cuts and save to use to make a pot of chili. The flavor from the bark of the brisket adds a great flavor to chili.

# Smoked Pork Butt

1 bone in medium sized pork shoulder (8-13 pounds)

1/4 to 1/2 cup of rub (depends on size of pork you use)

1/4 - 1/2 cup of seasoning rub (dry rub)

Smoker or grill that you can maintain a steady temperature on

Instant read meat thermometer

Water tray

Butcher or parchment paper

1. The first and one of the most important steps in this recipe is choosing a great pork butt from your store or butcher. I always go for a bone-in version that has a nice fat cap(thick white fleshy part).

2. Remove meat from plastic bag and make sure you give it a thorough rinse. Pat dry any excess water that remains on your pork shoulder. Lay out a few overlapping sheets of cling film. The cling film needs to be long enough to cover the pork shoulder. Place your pork shoulder on the cling film you laid out. Sprinkle your dry rub over all of the exposed meat on the pork shoulder. Make sure you get the rub into all of the crevasses and areas around the bone. It is not necessary to put rub on the fat cap but I always cover the whole piece of meat. Once your meat has been fully covered with the rub, wrap the shoulder with the cling film that it is sitting on. Place wrapped pork shoulder in a plastic bag so that it doesn't leak all over your kitchen. I like to keep mine in the fridge overnight before I smoke it, but if you are crunched for time you could let the shoulder sit for a minimum of 3-4 hours.

3. Get your smoker ready and bring it up to the proper temperature. I smoke my pork shoulder at 225 degrees F. I am currently using a pellet smoker for all my smoked BBQ. Some people prefer to use only lump coal or wood on their smokers. I say, use the grill you have and like to cook on. I like the pellet smoker because it allows me to do other things while I'm cooking. Maintaining a steady temperature on a grill can be complicated! Take your pork shoulder out of the fridge and let it come to room temperature.

4. Place your pork shoulder on your preheated smoker. Most of the time I place the pork in the grill fat side up, but if the smoker burns hot on the grill surface I place it fat side down to help shield the pork from the extra heat. Place the probe of the instant read thermometer in the thickest part of the center of the pork shoulder. Try to avoid getting the probe near any bones. If you have room in your smoker you should place a metal tray or tin of water. The water in the container will help keep some moisture in your smoker and keep your meat from drying out. Close your smoker and try to keep it closed as much as possible during the first few hours of the cook.

5. The time it will take you to finish your pork shoulder will depend on its size, the temperature of your smoker, and the ambient temperature to name a few things. I normally set aside 12 hours for a cut of meat this size, but the time could flex up or down depending on the day. Pork is well done at around 170 degrees F. You don't want to pull your pork shoulder at 170 degrees F. If you pull it at that temperature, your pork will be tough! However, I do pull my pork shoulder off the grill at 170 and I wrap it in Butcher or parchment paper. Some people like to wrap their pork in foil, but I don't like to use foil for mine. Once you have fully covered your pork in a wrap, place it back on your smoker and place the probe back in or near the same spot you removed it from.

# Smoked Pork Butt

6.  Once your shoulder has reached the temperature of 195-200 degrees F, pull it from your smoker and let it rest for a minimum of 25 minutes before you attempt to open up your wrapped pork.  If you are not serving the pork for a while you can place it in an empty cooler to ensure it maintains its temperature. If you smoked your shoulder properly, you should be able to shred it into bite size chunks with two kitchen forks. You can take the two forks and 'pull' in opposite directions. I like to serve my pork shoulder, pulled pork style. I pull all the skin that is left away from the meat. I scrape any fat that is left on the under side of the skin and mix it into the meat that I pull. A lot of the fat will melt away during the smoking process ,but there will be some left over to mix in with your pulled meat. I feel that the fat adds a great texture and moisture to the meat.

7.  The pork is great by itself, but you can add BBQ sauce to if you would like. I like to leave the BBQ sauce off so that my guest have the choice to put it on or leave it off.

8.  If you want to make a great sandwich using the pork from this recipe, add a few pickles to a bun of your choice and top with a handful of some of your pulled pork. Some people like to add coleslaw and BBQ sauce to their pulled pork sandwiches as well.

9.  This recipe is definitely an advanced recipe for those new to grilling/smoking. I feel that it will help you be a better cook in the kitchen if you can learn to smoke and grill food. The pork shoulder is a very forgiving cut of meat that isn't that expensive, so don't be scared to give this recipe a try a few times and lean how to customize it to make it your own! Happy Grilling!

# Time for Ribs

Earlier in the chapter about drinks, I spoke about dorm parties that me and my friends use to have. Our dorm parties started out huge but ultimately they evolved into monthly BBQ/DJ spin parties. In our dorm we had DJ's that covered a wide spectrum of different sounds that were popular. We would start off our parties low key with R&B music. While the R&B music would spin, we would get the BBQ grill going. We held our monthly parties on or near a payday. We knew that more people would be down to participate if it was near a payday. As our parties got better, so did our food. I started to cook ribs amongst other things. Most foods weren't that hard to come by on Okinawa, but good ribs were. Luckily for us, we were able to get ribs cheap from the commissary. It took me a few time cooking ribs before I got in my grove. I started to get a reputation for the guy that could cook ribs in my dorm. I never thought that I would become the "rib" guy. I wasn't even allowed to touch the grill when I was a child and now I was the go to guy for ribs! I was honored when people would ask me to cook ribs.

Word travels fast around the Air Force. After I left Okinawa, I was stationed in Germany for the first time. Some of the guys in my shop in Germany knew me or someone that knew me in Okinawa. We often had shop BBQ's when we had new people coming or a group of people leaving to go to their next base. We called the BBQ's/get togethers hail and farewells . The BBQ's were the basic hot dog and hamburger ones. One of the guys that knew me from Okinawa went to my supervisor after one of of our BBQ's and said that they should get me to cook at the next one. One day I was called into my supervisors office and he handed me a handful of cash. I asked him, "what is this for"? He told me that he had heard that I was "nice" on the BBQ grill, and he wanted me to make some ribs for the shop to help build morale. I was in the middle of a job. I said to him, "what about the unit that I am working on"? He said, "wrap that shit up and let's get some ribs on the grill"! I was shocked! I was happy and nervous at the same time. I mean, I had cooked for my friends a bunch, but cooking for a bunch of maintenance guys was intimidating! The ribs turned out great, and I had earned a permanent position as the shop grill master. I was a Senior Airman (E-3) at the time, so I didn't have much pull in my shop. I felt that my grill master status gave me a little bit of pull when it came to the higher ups (maybe that was just in my head).

I ended up coming back to Germany later in my career. I was at a different base but the guy that was my supervisor when I was in Germany the first time, was now in charge of the whole shop. It didn't take long before I got another handful of cash! I got a look from my shop chief when he gave me the money. He said, "you know what time it is"! Once again, I was back on the grill making ribs for a new group of maintainers. I was a supervisor and a Technical Sergeant (E-6) this time around, so things had changed a bit. I often feel that the more things change, the more they remain the same. In this case, I was happy that my status of the shop grill master was still intact!

# Typical Shop BBQ

During one of our typical maintenance shop BBQ's, I would start by prepping our shop BBQ pit. I tried to focus most of my efforts on trying to make sure the ribs and other meats were cooked properly. I always used charcoal in lieu of wood because it was always available and the cook times were predictable.  Cooking for a lot of people can have its challenges but it definitely gets easier the more you do it.

I normally made all the meats, my baked beans and a few sides. Other people from my shop would either buy sides and desserts or have their spouses bring in something.

The morale that came from having shop BBQ's was always a needed boost for all of us!

# Smoked Ribs

**2-4 Racks of St Louis-style Spare Ribs**

**Basic BBQ Rub (recipe at the start of this chapter)**

**Grill preheated to 250° F**

**Mustard**

**Apple Cider Vinegar (in a spray bottle)**

At the top of this picture, you can see the membrane that were removed from the two racks of ribs I was smoking.

1.  Prep ribs by removing the membrane from the back of the ribs.  Rinse ribs with water and pat dry with paper towels. I prefer to cook my ribs without the membrane because they tend to be more tender when they are done. I also don't like how tough the membrane gets after cooking the ribs.

2.  Rub in a thin layer of mustard on both sides of the ribs. Sprinkle dry rub over both sides of ribs. At this point you could cook your ribs, but I prefer to wrap mine in cling film and let them sit in the refrigerator for 8-12 hours. Remove from the refrigerator and allow to reach room temperature before cooking.

3.  Place ribs on preheated grill or smoker that is at 250° F. Make sure that the ribs are not placed over direct heat. The ribs should cook low and slow.  Use the apple cider vinegar to mist the ribs when the start to dry out during the cooking process.

4.  It will normally take anywhere from 3-4 hours for the ribs to finish cooking. You will know that the ribs are done when the meat starts to pull away from the bones.

5.  Halfway through the cooking process I take my ribs off the grill and wrap in foil or butcher paper. After I wrap them I put them back on the grill. The wrap helps keep the ribs nice and tender.  This step is optional!

6.  I don't put any BBQ sauce on anything I BBQ until I am almost ready to pull the meat off the grill. BBQ sauce often causes fire flare ups due to all of the sugar that is typically in the sauce. If you like to add sauce, make it the last step of the cooking process.

7.  Let ribs rest for 10-15 minuets after removing from the grill before you serve them.

# Balcony Steaks*

**1-4 well marbled ribeye steaks( 8-16 once each)**

**Salt**

**Pepper**

**Garlic powder**

**paprika**

**Preheated grill**

**Salted Butter**

**Metal tongs**

* I made steaks for my in-laws once, when I lived in Germany. The house that we lived in had multiple levels. I kept my grill on the balcony because it was the level the kitchen was on. My sister-in-law liked the steak I made her and till this day she refers to my grilled steaks as "balcony steaks".

1. Take steaks out of the refrigerator and season generously with salt, pepper, garlic powder, & paprika. Make sure you season all sides of the meat.

2. Cover steaks and let sit outside of the refrigerator until they reach room temperature.

3. While your steaks are climatizing, check your grill to make sure you have it hot enough. If you are cooking on a charcoal grill, it's best if your coals are white hot. If your coals are new, you will get a strong coal taste that might make the meat taste bad. I like to get the grill as hot as I can, so I make sure I get a good sear on the outside of the steaks. Gas grills cut out a lot of the guesswork ,but you might miss the flavor that wood or coal can add.

4. Place steaks on grill over direct fire. Cook 1-2 minutes per side, depending on the thickness. When you turn the steaks make sure you let the fire sear the sides as well.  You will more than likely have a few fire flare-ups depending on how fatty the steaks are. Be sure to monitor the flare-ups to ensure the steaks don't get burned.

5. Once steaks are browned to your likeness, remove from direct heat and continue to cook until they reach your desired doneness. I cook my steaks to medium rare (135° F).

6. Remove from heat and let rest for about 10 minutes. Place a slice of butter on top of the steaks and season with a little salt while they rest.

7. Best served fresh with roasted vegetables and potatoes!

# Schwenkbraten

1 large onion

1 shallot

2 tsp smoked paprika

1 tsp dried marjoram

1 tsp dried oregano

1/2 tsp pepper

1 tsp sea salt

1 tbsp of minced garlic

2 tbsp of stone ground mustard

1 tbsp of juniper berries

Charcoal grill with beechwood or long charcoal

I took this photo at a wine festival in Bernkasel-Kues, Germany. The gentleman in the photo over the fire pit was hard at work grilling Schwenkbraten's. The key to getting the traditional taste has a bit to do with the swinging grill( Schwenker) and the beechwood that is used to produce the signature flavor. I don't own a swinging grill and I have never actually used beechwood to cook mine at home, but I have come pretty damn close to recreating one of my favorite dishes from the Rhineland Pfalz region of Germany!

1.    Add sea salt, oregano, marjoram, paprika, juniper berries and pepper into a food processor. Pulse the processor until all ingredients are properly mixed.

2.    Peel and slice onion and shallot into thin slices. Place onions, minced garlic, and shallot into a gallon size sealable bag.

3.    Rub blended spices into pork steaks. Make sure that all surfaces are covered. Place pork steaks into the bag with the onions in it. Give the bag a good shake so that the garlic, shallots, and onions are nicely mixed in with the pork steaks. Try to get as much air as you can out of the bag. Seal the bag and place in a refrigerator for at least 6 hours. I like to leave mine in the refrigerator overnight.

4.    Prepare your BBQ grill for a three zone fire. The three zone fire will help keep the steaks from cooking too fast and help replicate the idea of having a swinging grill (or Schwenker). The coals toward the top of the grill will be the hottest zone. If you have a good slope of coals in your grill, you should have a high, medium and low heat area in your grill.  While the fire in your grill is coming together, be sure to take your steaks out of the refrigerator and let come to room temperature.

5.    Pull your steaks from the bag you had them marinating in. It is not necessary to pull out the onions. If a few onions are stuck to your steaks , it should be fine. Place your steaks on your grill in the hottest zone in order to sear and lock in the flavors of the steaks. You will need to flip and rotate the steaks as needed. I normally cook the steaks for about 3-4 minutes on each side in the hottest area or the grill, then I move the steaks in and out of the different cooking zones as needed. Be sure to watch out for flare-ups. Flare ups can cause your meat to cook too fast in some areas. The minimum recommended temperature to cook pork to is 145 degrees F. I normally have an instant read thermometer on hand anytime I cook meat, but after you cook a few of these you will be able to tell when your steaks are done based off the feel of the steaks on your kitchen tongs.  Once your steaks are done, it is best to consume immediately. In Germany, you typically see people eat Schwenkbraten on a fresh Brotchen (German Roll) .

# BBQ Chicken

**2-4 lbs of Chicken (I like a mix of wings and drums)**

**For Marinade:**

**2 tbsp of lemon or lime juice**

**2 tsp Garlic Powder**

**2 tsp Paprika**

**2 tsp Sea Salt**

**2 tsp Minced Garlic**

**2 tsp Black Pepper**

**2 tbsp Olive Oil**

**3 tsp Mustard Powder**

1. Mix all ingredients except for chicken in a bowl. When everything is mixed together nicely, set aside. The measurements above are more of a guideline when it comes to the dry ingredients. Add more or less based on your taste.

2. Rinse chicken with cool water and pat dry with paper towels.

3. Pour marinade over chicken and rub in thoroughly. Once all pieces of chicken are coated, place in a sealed container and store in the refrigerator for a minimum of 6 hours. I like to store the chicken overnight. Remove chicken about 30 minutes before you want to grill it.

4. Set your grill up for indirect heat. I like to use lump charcoal because it burns hot and long. Not all lump charcoal taste good, so make sure you pick one with good flavor. The charcoal you use can throw off the flavor of your chicken. Make sure that you let your grill come up to heat for 20-30 minutes before you begin cooking.

5. Once the grill is up to heat and you have a clean burn coming off your coals, you are ready to cook.

6. Place chicken on the grill away from the direct heat. If you grill the chicken over direct fire it will cook the outside too fast. Cover the grill if you have a cover and make sure the vents are fully open.

7. Check and rotate chicken as needed. The chicken will be done between 30- 50 minutes. Some grills will cook faster than others. If you are new to BBQ, you might want to get a nice instant read thermometer so that you can check the temp of your chicken. Your chicken is done when it reaches 165 degrees F internally.

# BBQ Grilled Beans

**2 large cans of baked beans (drained)**

**1 large onion chopped small**

**1 pound of ground meat**

**6-8 slices of bacon (cooked and cut into small chunks)**

**1 cup of bbq sauce of your choice (I normally use hickory or honey bbq sauce)**

**Season salt**

**Garlic powder**

**1/2 cup of packed brown sugar**

**Preheated grill or smoker**

1. Sauté onions in a large pan. When onions are almost translucent, add ground beef and brown while chopping it into small chunks. Sprinkle garlic powder and season salt on meat while it's cooking.

2. When your meat has fully cooked through, remove it from stove and drain excess fat.

3. Put beans in a 13x9 baking dish. Add in meat and onion mixture, bacon, bbq sauce, and brown sugar. Mix everything together and taste the sauce to see if you would like to add anything else (like pepper or peppers).

4. Place beans on your grill away from direct heat. Grill until beans come to a slow simmer. Everything in the dish is already cooked but you want to keep it on the grill for a bit to help all of the flavors marry.

5. This is my base recipe for grilled beans but I like to change it up at times and add different meats depending on what I am cooking that day. Pulled pork and brisket also mix well with this dish.

I like to use disposable pans when I BBQ baked beans because clean up is easy and you don't have to worry about the grill messing up one of your good pans.

# 焼鳥 (Yakitori)

Street food is prevalent in many cultures. My first exposer to street food was at the fair when I was a kid. I use to love going to the fair because it was a time of year that I could eat food that wasn't normally on any menu in a restaurant. I also loved the fact that most of the food at the fair was cheap compared to going to restaurant.

In Okinawa, I use to go to this place called the Sunabe Sea Wall on some weekends and nights off that I had. There was shopping plaza that wasn't that far from the sea wall that use to have different types of Japanese street foods. At first I was reluctant to try some of the foods in the streets because it was just too new for me. After I had been on the island a few months, I warmed up to the idea of trying some of the food. I saw this guy standing next to what looked like a small pushable ice cream cart. It wasn't an ice cream cart though. In fact it was a portable grill. This day and age a portable grill doesn't sound too impressive ,but let me tell you this thing was state of the art. The most impressive part about this grill was that it was a charcoal grill. The charcoal that the guy was using was like nothing I had ever seen in the south. It was white hot, and it barely put off any smoke or ashes, but still smelled amazing. I later found out that he was using coal made from a wood called Binchōtan. This coal made from oak trees that grow in Japan is unique to Japanese cuisine.

The street vendor was preparing Yakitori. At the time I had no idea what yakitori was but I know it looked and smelled amazing. I asked my friends what he was cooking and the vendor chimed in with his own response, "Chicken", he said with a grin on his face. I was like well damn, I'm always down for some chicken! I told him that I would take two of the skewers. What happened after I placed my order made me realize things are done way different in Japan (in a good way). The vendor sprung into action like his reputation was on the line. He grabbed two skewers with chicken and gently placed them on his grill. He already had a few cooking that he continued to monitor. I was in awe at how poised the street vendor was under the pressure of a bunch of hungry, tipsy Americans eagerly waiting on their chicken to get done. I don't think I even spoke while I was watching him prepare my chicken. I loved the dedication that he had to make sure my food was perfect. Towards the end of the cooking process the vendor covered my chicken skewers with a sauce before he put them on a serving plate. I looked the man in his eyes and said thank you. He looks back at me and said "Please Try" with a serious look on his face! This man stared me down like his whole reputation was on the line, based on how I felt about his chicken. I tried the Yakitori and it was out of this world! I think I said something along the lines of "damn, that's some bomb ass chicken"! The serious look on the Japanese vendors face changed to one of accomplishment. I doubt the vendor understood what my comment meant. All he needed to know was that I had already pretty much "breathed" in the first skewer in like 10 seconds! He bowed to me and I returned the bow. Since that day, I have a special place in my heart for Yakitori.

On my last trip to Japan ,I stopped at many spots for my fill of Yakitori. My wife and I also had a few skewered pieces of Kobe beef (Yakiniku) in Tokyo. As soon I returned from Japan, I was on a mission to recreate Yakitori. I asked myself, why should I have to wait to go to Japan to eat one of my favorite chicken dishes? I know that my recipe might not be as authentic as the ones that I've tasted in Japan, but I hope to be able to bring the same level of enjoyment that I had when I first tried Yakitori to anyone tasting or remaking my recipe. Photos below show a good representation of the variety of skewered meats you can have in Japan. These photos are from my last trip to Tokyo.

# Yakitori

2 -3 chicken thighs with skin on (organic)

3-4 stalks of green onions

Wood Skewers

Salt and Pepper

Garlic Powder

Preheated grill*

1. Cut chicken thighs into small chucks( about 2 x 1 inch in size)

2. Cut the bottom part of the white stalk off of the green onions. Cut green onions a little bigger than an inch long starting from the bottom up.  I try to only use the firm sections of the green onion.

3. Alternate green onions and chunks of chicken on the wooden skewers(see picture). I like to try to get about 4-5 pieces of chicken and onion per skewer.

4. Season each skewer with salt, pepper and garlic powder to your taste. I don't think they use garlic powder in Japan, but I  like the taste it adds to this dish.

5.  Place skewers on preheated grill.  Gently cook all sides ensuring chicken is cooked thru but not burned. Rotate chicken skewers to cooler parts of your grill if they seem to be cooking too fast.

6. Ideally, your chicken should be slightly crispy on the outside and juicy on the inside.

7. Its optional to add sauce to your Yakitori. I prefer mine with sauce.  The yakitori sauce recipe is available a few pages ahead.

* Traditionally Yakitori is cooked over an open grill that uses Kishu Binchotan charcoal. This type of charcoal comes directly from japan. You can find Binchotan online but it won't be cheap. Some of the main benefits of this type of coal is that is burns clean and hot for a long time. A little bit of this Charcoal will go a long way. If you aren't ready to drop cash on this exclusive Charcoal, make sure you use a clean burning heat source. You don't want to overpower the taste of your Yakitori with heavy smoke.

Kishu Binchotan charcoal

# Yakitori Sauce

Yakitori can been eaten with or without sauce. I prefer to eat mine with sauce because that is how it was first introduced to me.

| Ingredient | Amount | |
|---|---|---|
| Soy sauce | 4 | Ounces |
| Mirin | 4 | Ounces |
| Brown Sugar | 2 | TBSP |
| Crushed garlic | 3 | Cloves |
| Green onion | 1 | Stalk chopped |
| Corn starch | 1 | TBSP |
| Water | 2 | TBSP |

1. Add soy sauce, mirin, brown sugar, crush garlic and green onion to a medium size sauce pan on medium high heat.

2. Mix corn starch and water together. Set aside.

3. Bring sauce to a boil and allow to cook for about 5 minutes.

4. Remove sauce from the heat and pour through a strainer into bowl. This will separate the garlic and onion from the sauce. Return strained sauce to the sauce pan.

5. Place sauce pan back on the stove on medium low heat. Add the corn starch mixture to the sauce and continue cooking over low heat for 1-2 minutes. The sauce should thicken up.

6. Remove from heat and set aside until you are ready to use on your yakitori.

# Chapter 4
# Mains

Choosing a main dish for dinner can be a bit of a difficult task. The main dish has a huge responsibility to meet all of your expectations. I often get upset when I go out to eat and I order the wrong main course. If I get the wrong main, I feel like I wasted my chance at having an amazing dish. I find myself looking around at other people's tables having buyers remorse because I choose the wrong main dish.

When I was deciding what I would include in this chapter, I didn't have a price point in mind. I wanted to place items in this chapter that could hold their own as a main dish regardless of how big the meal is. Quantity does not always equate to quality in regards to having a good main dish.

Many of the dishes in this chapter are regionally based. Some of the dishes that are in this chapter are not well known and I wouldn't be surprised if some of you are hearing about these dishes for the first time. When I speak

to people that are from different parts of the world, I often ask them "what is something that a lot of people eat where you are from"?

I was fortunate enough be able to travel around and get to experience main dishes from all parts of the world. I will continue to eat and try to learn how to make different mains from places I visit.

Some of the dishes in this chapter can stand on their own without the need for any sides. I encourage you to fix and use any recipe in this book how you see fit. I try not to get so caught up in titles when it comes to food. I categorized the recipes in this book for organizational purposes only.

I hope that you can learn to make and love the recipes in this chapter as much as I do. Feel free to experiment and add your own additions to help the recipe's cater to you and your guest if need be.

# MAINS

ZURCHER GESCHNETZELTES

BEER BRATS

CHEESY EGG DROP RAMEN

SLOW COOKER BARBACOA

RAHMSNITZEL

WHITE BEAN CHILI

LASAGNA

CHOPPED CHEESE

TACO RICE

BEEF ENCHILADAS

SHRIMP & GRITS

FISH TACOS

CHICKEN KATSU CURRY

BRAISED OXTAILS

# Zürcher Geschnetzeltes

I took this picture of one of my favorite dishes that I ate in Germany. The fist time I ever had it was during a trip to Baden-Baden with my wife. We scheduled a weekend getaway to visit one of Bavaria's favorite spa towns. The town of Baden-Baden is amazing! The first night that we arrived in Baden-Baden it was late and there wasn't a lot of places open to eat at. We decided to go eat at Lowenbräu. I told the waitress, I wanted something different that wasn't Schnitzel. She recommended that I try this dish. I didn't know what I was in store for but I heard her say it had veal and gravy, so I was sold!

Funny thing is, this dish actually is a traditional meal from Switzerland. I never actually ordered this meal when I was in Switzerland but I did eat other tasty meals there. I just love the amount of flavor this dish packs! The item that looks like a big hash brown is called a Rösti. The pot on the left that looks like a pot of gravy is a delicious mixture of seared veal that is combined with a mushroom gravy and creme fraiche.

# Zürcher Geschnetzetzeltes

| | |
|---|---|
| 1 pound of veal cutlets (sliced) | paprika |
| 1 large Shallot diced | Olive oil |
| 8 ounces of heavy cream | 2 tbsp butter |
| 1 cup of white wine | 1 tbsp of flour |
| 1/2 cup of vegetable or beef stock | 4 ounces of fresh sliced mushrooms |
| salt & pepper | 1 tbsp of cornstarch mixed with water (if needed) |

1. Preheat a large skillet over medium heat. Once your skillet is hot, add about 2 tablespoons of olive oil. Season veal with salt, paprika and pepper to taste. Sear sliced veal pieces on all sides, making sure not to overcook. Your veal might be a little pink in the center but it will continue cooking in your sauce later. Place seared veal and most of the juice it created into a bowl and set aside.

2. Sauté the shallots until they are translucent but not burnt. Add butter and mushrooms and cook until they become tender. Add flour and stir until it it starts to brown. Make sure that you stir flour around the pan good and don't let it stick.

3. Add wine to skillet to deglaze all of the flavor. Make sure you scape all sides of the pan to ensure you capture all of the season and flavor. Add stock to pan and bring to a slow simmer. Add heavy cream and stir until cream is incorporated. Return veal and its juices back to your pan and continue to cook for about 10 minutes at low heat. If you would like the sauce to be thicker you can add the cornstarch mixture to help thicken but this is totally up to you.

4. This dish is best served the traditional way over a potato Rösti ,but can be enjoyed what ever way you see fit. The Rösti recipe is located in the sides chapter.

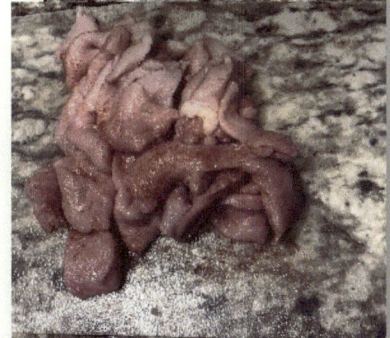

# Beer Brats

For as long as I can remember, I have been a Green Bay Packers fan. My father was a Chicago Bears fan being that he was from Chicago, but I never liked the Bears. I became a Packers fan because they are the number one rivals to the Chicago Bears. When we use to watch the games on TV, they would show tailgaters cooking outside the stadiums. I remember seeing hot dogs and burgers but the dish that caught my eye the most was beer brats!

I think the reason why I was so intrigued by the beer brats were because they had beer in them.

I can't remember my father ever making them for us, but I was able to taste them on my travels to Chicago to visit him. One summer we took a family member to Wisconsin. I believe that trip to Wisconsin was the first time I ever had beer brats. It was love at first bite! I loved that the fact that the bun soaked up all of the flavor from the juice that came off the brat. The onions and peppers added a depth of flavor that took things to a whole other level. The beer that bound all the flavors together brought out the robust flavors of the ingredients.

Till this day, beer brats hold a special place in my heart! I love to make them for big games or when I know we are having folks over the house for a party or something.

A few years ago I went to a wedding of a family member in Wisconsin. The day before the wedding, we were hanging out at the home of the bride. Everyone was hungry and we were all trying to decide what we could eat that would be enough to feed everyone. My wife and I went

Cooking beer brats for a group of people in Wisconsin.

to to the store and the thought of cooking brats came to my head. I was nervous to cook them! At this point in my life I had made brats many of times, but I have never made brats for a bunch of people from Wisconsin, in Wisconsin! I was on edge! I was in a kitchen that wasn't mine (pictured), using a grill that I had never used before, cooking for people I just met, and trying to hold a conversation and be social! On the surface I was cool but I was freaking out on the inside.

In the end, everyone told me they enjoyed the brats. I think I went around asking everyone for feedback like 2 or three times. I felt if people from Wisconsin don't like my beer brats, then I am doing something wrong and I need to go back to the drawing board.

In any case, I hope that you enjoy my beer brat recipe!

# Beer Brats

**5-10 Bratwurst (brats)**

**2 bell peppers cored and sliced ( I like to use two colors if possible)**

**Salt and pepper**

**3 garlic cloves minced**

**2 large yellow onions thinly sliced**

**Paprika**

**Hoagie rolls**

**2 12 ounce beers (I prefer to use German Hefeweizen)**

**2 Tbsp of butter**

**Preheated grill**

1.  Place butter in a large deep pan over medium heat. Sauté onions until they are almost translucent. Add bell peppers and continue to sauté until peppers are soft any beginning to caramelize. Season pan with salt and pepper to taste. Add minced garlic and be sure to stir everything together. Remove from heat for now.

2. Place brats on your preheated grill. You want to make sure that you give your brats a nice sear on the out side. Be sure not to burn the brats. If your grill begins to flame up, you will need to move the brats out of direct heat.  If you don't have a grill, you can sear in a separate skillet.

3. Once the brats have a nice char on all sides, put them to the coolest side of the grill. The brats will more than likely still be raw in the middle. Don't worry about the brats only being cooked on the outside. The brats will continue to cook in the beer.

4.  Return onions and peppers to the heat on your stove or grill and bring to a sizzle. Once you have a nice hot sizzle, pour in the beer. Bring beer to a nice slow simmer and add in the brats.

5. Continue to cook brats until most of the liquid has cooked out of your pan.  During this time, I like to taste the liquid in the pan and add in the paprika and any more salt and pepper I think the dish needs.

6. To serve: Open a hoagie roll and place some of your onions and peppers inside (I put them in first to keep them from falling off). Place one of the brats on top of the peppers and onions and top with mustard.

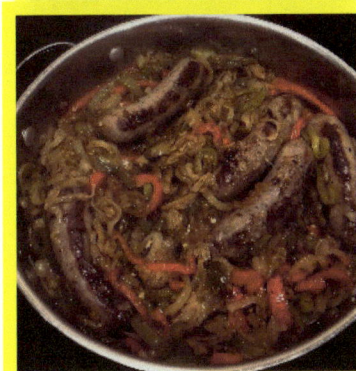

# Ramen

Growing up there were a few things that we pretty much always had in the cabinets to cook. One of the items that I knew I could rely on if there wasn't anything else to eat was instant ramen! I can't even begin to count how many times I have cooked ramen. I use to think that I was the only one that ate ramen as frequent as I did until I got older. I spoke to many of my military friends that were from all parts of the world and they all for the most part could remember eating instant ramen. I never liked the microwave version of instant ramen. I feel that it did not get hot enough and the flavors never really blend like they do when you cook on the stove.

My dad originally taught me how to make instant ramen. I know most of you are thinking that making instant ramen is easy. I will agree that making instant ramen is easy, but if you are simply following the directions on the packet you are not experiencing the full potential of what you could make. Every since I have been making instant ramen the way my dad taught me, I have never looked back.

These days, I prefer to eat at Japanese Ramen places if I have a craving for ramen. I still like to eat my cheesy egg drop ramen from time to time as a quick go to meal!

# Cheesy Egg Drop Ramen

1 package (3 OZ) of instant ramen

1 egg

1 slice of American cheese

Hot sauce

1. Bring 2 cups of water to a rolling boil. You can use less water if you want your soup base thicker.

2. Add noodle block to boiling water(I break mine in half before I put it in the water). Turn heat down medium.

3. Stir noodles and make sure that they are cooked thoroughly. I normally let mine cook about 4 minutes. Add season pack and remove from heat. Stir season until it is mixed in.

4. Turn heat down to low. Return pot to heat. Crack egg open and add to noodle mixture. Stir egg quickly making sure that you break the yoke in the process. The egg will begin to cook. You want to make sure that you stir the egg throughout the pot so that you don't have a bunch of clumps.

5. Once the egg has cooked remove pot from the heat. Add the slice of American cheese to the top of the noodle mixture. Stir the noodles until the cheese is completely melted.

6. Pour contents into a bowl and eat immediately. Top with your favorite hot sauce if you want.

This dish may not be for everyone, but it is ideal for any budget!

# Slow Cooker Beef Barbacoa

# Slow Cooker Beef Barbacoa

**2 packs of beef cheek( 2-4 lbs)**

**4-5 cloves of garlic peeled**

**2 bay leaves**

**1 large onion chopped**

**2 tbsp of salt**

**1 tbsp of pepper**

**1 tbsp of ground cumin**

**Juice of 1 lime**

**Large slow cooker**

1. Rinse beef cheeks with cool water and trim off excess fat. The cheeks have a lot of fat hanging from them and you won't be able to trim all of it. The important fat to trim is the fat that is not attached to the meat directly.

2. Place beef cheeks in slow cooker and season with salt, pepper, and cumin. Place chopped onions, bay leaves and garlic cloves in slow cooker.

3. Pour lime juice over meat and place heat on high. Be sure to keep your slow cooker covered. Cook on high for 8 hours, being sure to check and stir every few hours.

4. My slow cooker has a function that keeps contents warm for a few hours after the 8 hour mark. I normally leave the meat in the slow cooker until I am ready to serve it.

5. To serve: Drain excess fat and shred meat into edible chunks. This meat is great on tacos, burritos, enchiladas or tortas!

When I was stationed in New Mexico(right near the Texas Border), I would always get a beef Barbacoa Torta(Mexican sandwich) from the burrito food truck that came on base. My supervisor was Mexican and he put me on to Barbacoa. I had heard of it before but never thought to try it until he ordered it one day. I was hooked after I had my first taste! There are restaurants and chains that claim to have Barbacoa on their menu. If you have had "real" Tex Mex Barbacoa, you'll know that it's hard to find outside of Texas. I tried to get this recipe as close as I could, without having the traditional underground pit needed to make this properly. I hope you like it as much as I do!

# Rahmschnitzel

The first time I had Rahmschnitzel, I didn't even know what it was! I saw it on someones plate and thought it looked good, so I asked the waiter what it was. This dish immediately became one of my favorite meals to have in Germany! Not everyone makes it the same and it varies based on what region you get it in.

# Rahmschnitzel (fried breaded meat in cream sauce)

**1 small onion chopped**

**Salt , pepper and paprika to taste**

**2-3 slices of chopped pancetta or Canadian bacon**

**3-4 tablespoons of butter**

**2 tablespoons of flour plus more for breading**

**1 small container of fresh whipping cream**

**1/4 cup of water**

**4-6 ounces of sour cream**

**1 small can of mushrooms (optional)**

**4 boneless pork or veal escalopes**

1. Melt butter over medium heat in a large pan. Add onions, bacon or pancetta and sauté until you have a nice golden brown color.

2. Add 2 tablespoons of flour to your pan and mix it in with the contents of the pan. Add 1/4 cup of water to the pan and give it a good stir.

3. Add sour cream and whipping cream and bring to a boil for about 5 minutes. Check sauce for taste and add salt and pepper as needed. Reduce heat to low and simmer.

4. Use a meat tenderizer to help veal or pork flatten out.

5. Season meat with salt, pepper and paprika. Lightly bread meat with flour.

6. Heat oil in a separate skillet or pan over medium high heat. Add meat and fry on both sides until lightly brown.

7. Transfer fried meat to the pan with the cream sauce and simmer for 20-30 minutes or until meat is cooked thru (which ever comes first).

8. For best results serve immediately. anything with a cream sauce is best served fresh in my opinion.

Normally schnitzel is served with potatoes, noodles or home fries in Germany. Some places serve schnitzel with spaetzle and gravy.

# Chili

The first time I made chili was in a home economics class at in middle school. I didn't want to even be in home etc class at first. I didn't see the point of sewing and all that other stuff they had us doing. I was happy about the cooking part. The bad part was it wasn't "just" a cooking class. Anyway, we were first taught how to make a basic chili in our separate kitchens with our team. Once our teacher knew that we all knew the basics of how to make chili, she told us that we would have a chili cook off, based on our own recipes. I am always down for some friendly competition, so the idea of a cook off was very exiting to me. I remember having some creative differences with the team I was assigned to. They wanted to make it hot. My thought process was, why are we going to add all of these ingredients to our chili just to make it so hot we can't taste them. I felt that it was a massive waste of our time. We made our chili and gave it to teachers along with all the others that competed. We lost! I wasn't surprised. We had a great base, ingredients, and consistency but it was so hot that most of that was lost when our judges tasted our entry.

I learned some very valuable lessons about cooking for other people during that chili cook off. One of those lessons is just because you like how something taste, doesn't mean that the majority of people will. I always want different people to try my food, and I always ask them how does it taste? I immediately say after I ask how it taste, "Do you think I need to add anything to it"? I don't even care if the people I ask know anything about food. I get mad when someone devalues someones opinion just because they aren't trained in the thing they are judging. Sometimes the best critics are the ones that aren't blinded by what they think something should taste like.

Chili is still one of my favorite comfort foods to make! These days I am more about it being consistently good every time I make it. The JROTC program that I teach for has a chili cook-off every October in conjunction with a military style change of command. We swap out leadership 2 times a year. The other change of command is more formal, but I enjoy the chili cook-off a little more simply because it involves cooking and competition. I have made chili for our annual chili cook-off but I don't enter mine into the competition. I don't need a prize for my food, I just want to know that people enjoy it. The first two years I was at the school, I was part of the judging panel. I was happy that everyone got a vote in the last few years. I feel that everyone should have a voice when it comes to the flavor of food, not just a select few. Plus, it was hard on my stomach eating all that chili.

The last time I entered a chili competition was when I was stationed at RAF (Royal Air Force) Fairford, in England. There wasn't many people stationed on this base, so everyone on base knew each other. Even if you didn't personally know someone, you knew where they worked and their name. I made a white bean chili with rotisserie duck meat and a regular chili that I called the 5 meat wonder. The five meat wonder had chicken thighs, Italian sausage, bacon, steak, and ground beef. I figured if I entered two pots of chili into the competition, there was no way I wasn't walking away with a prize. Some people knew what chili I made but others had no idea. The judges that were picked for that competition were top ranking officials on the base. I was a little upset when I found out about how it would be judged. I remember asking one of my friends "what the heck do these kats know about chili bruh"? I understand it was a respect thing because the judges held high powered positions on the base, but none of them were Chefs or even home cooks as far as I knew. The event was cool and everyone got to chill and eat chili for about an hour. When the results came in I was hella nervous. I really care about my food and what others think of it. I didn't win! I was pissed. I had tried all the other pots of chili entered and I didn't feel that I could lose. My friends were all surprised I didn't win! I walked over to gather my stuff and I realized that both of my pots of chili were empty! Most of the other pots of chili were over half full still. I had multiple people that were in the crowd approach me and tell me that my chili was the best that they tasted. I realized at that point that even though I didn't win a prize for my chili, I earned the praise and respect from the general populace on the base. I felt like I was the peoples champ that day. I learned more from my loss than I would have if I won that day. I haven't entered another chili competition since but I know a lot of folks have enjoyed chili that I've made.

# White Bean Chili

1 Carroll Shelby's White Chicken Chili kit (or your preferred chili kit)

1 15.5 OZ can of Cannelloni beans(drained)

1 pound of sweet Italian Sausage(uncased)

1 Pound of Boneless\skinless chicken thighs

1 onion

1 green bell pepper

2 cups of chicken stock(unsalted)

1 cup of water

Fresh sliced corn on the cob(optional)

1. Cut chicken into small dice( about 1 inch). It really doesn't matter how big you cut the chicken but I use the small method to ensure there is chicken throughout the chili. Once chicken is cut season with season salt.

2. Dice onions and green peppers. Slice corn kernels off 2 ears of fresh corn(optional).

3. Heat a large pot or dutch oven over medium high heat. Add about a TBSP of oil and the diced peppers and onions. Sauté your mixture until the peppers are soft and the onions are almost translucent. Add the chicken and sausage you prepared and cook until it has been cooked throughout and browned. I like to break the sausage down so that I know that it is fully cooked and to help it disperse better in the chili.

4. Add chicken stock and water to your pot and give it a good stir. At this point I also add the large spice pack that comes in the chili kit. I season to my taste, so I don't use the salt and pepper pack that comes with the chili kit. I only add the flour if I want my chili to be thicker. I use this chili kit because it gives you great versatility.

5. Cook at medium low heat for about 30 minutes or so. Add beans in the last 10 minutes. I like to serve this chili as is but you could also add some shredded sharp cheddar cheese and sour cream if that's how you get down. The Chili pictured is not as thick as I normally make. Please remember that the chili will thicken up after it has cooled. If the chili has too much liquid, you can cook it longer without a lid to allow some of the liquid to boil off.

# Lasagna

Red Sauce (see note)

1 pound of Italian sausage

I pound of ground beef

Cottage cheese

Lasagna

Mozzarella cheese (16 once bag minimum)

Parmigiana Cheese (grated)

1 Large onion diced

Fresh basil leaves

*Note: I use my red sauce for multiple things that I cook. It's a nice versatile sauce that works for all types of dishes. See next page for recipe.*

1. Brown onion, Italian sausage and ground beef. Drain meat mixture and add to a medium pot with red sauce. Bring sauce to medium heat and allow to cool down a bit.

2. Boil Lasagna until it is al dente. I recommend you add seat salt and a few tablespoons of olive oil to your boiling water. I always season my pasta water because the pasta takes on the taste of the water as it boils. Once pasta has finished boiling, drain your pot and be sure to separate your pasta so that it doesn't stick together.

3. Take a small amount of the sauce mixture and spread it across the bottom of a 13" x 9" casserole pan. You don't need to put a thick layer of sauce. This first layer of sauce both flavors the bottom of your lasagna and keeps it from sticking to your pan. Place three pieces of lasagna pasta side by side lengthwise on top of the thin layer of red sauce mix. On the top of the pasta that you just placed will be the first full layer of your dish. Start by putting an even level of sauce until the pasta is covered. Now cover the layer of sauce with cottage cheese (I like to use a spatula to ensure everything is smoothed out). Cover the cottage cheese with a generous sprinkle of mozzarella cheese. Tear some of your basil leaves into small pieces and place on top of your layers of cheese. At this point you have completed one layer. I normally do a minimum of 3 full layers before I complete my top layer.

4. The top layer is a little different from the rest of the layers. I like to call the top layer the "cheese shelf" because its main purpose in the dish is to complete the layering of the lasagna and it also holds the majority of the cheese that creates a delicious seal. Place the final layer of pasta on top and cover with enough sauce to cover the pasta. Cover the top with mozzarella cheese until you can't see any of your sauce. Sprinkle freshly grated parmigiana cheese on the top. You can put as much as you like. I normally use about 1/2 cup.

5. Place lasagna in a preheated 375 degree F oven. You can cover your lasagna with aluminum foil for the first 23 or so minutes if you chose to. I prefer not to cover mine. If you do decide to cover, make sure you remove the foil cover so that your cheese on top can brown. Overall, I would leave the lasagna in the oven long enough for all your cheese to cook to your preferred doneness.

# Red Sauce

2 28 ounce cans of peeled Italian Roma tomatoes

2 cups of water

1/3 cup of tomato paste

3 ounces of olive oil

2 large cloves of garlic diced

Salt and pepper

1 tsp garlic powder

Fresh basil

Italian seasoning

1 tbsp of sugar

1. Heat olive oil over medium heat in a large pot. Once oil has come up to temperature place diced garlic in and cook until golden brown.

2. Place tomato paste in pot and cook for about 1-2 minutes. Make sure that you stir the tomato paste thoroughly. The paste will change color slightly. Make sure that the paste doesn't stick to the pot.

3. Add the 2 cans of tomatoes to the pot and stir. Use a hand immersion blender to chop up the tomatoes. If you don't have a hand blender, you can use a food processor to chop up the tomatoes to your desired consistency. Make sure that the paste is fully mixed in with the tomatoes. Add in the two cups of water and salt and pepper to taste. Add garlic powder and give the sauce a big stir. Tear or chop basil leaves and place in sauce. The amount of basil leaves(I typically use 10) you use is totally up to you.

4. Reduce heat to a low simmer and stir in sugar and Italian seasoning. It's a good idea to place a lid over your pot while cooking to prevent sauce from splattering all over your kitchen. You have to be careful to not let too much condensation drip into the pot because it can make your sauce to watery.

5. Continue to monitor and stir your sauce as needed for about 30 minutes to an hour. Before you turn off the heat taste your sauce to make sure it is to your liking.

6. I use this cause as a base for many of my pasta dishes that require a red sauce. If you are going to use this sauce for ziti or lasagna, be sure that you keep the sauce on the thicker side.

# CHOPPED CHEESE SANDWICH

The first time I heard the name "chopped cheese" I didn't know what it meant. I was listening to one of my favorite rap artist "Camron" (AKA Killa Cam) and he mentioned a steak and cheese sandwich in his song "Child of the Ghetto". Camron filmed his video for Child of the Ghetto inside a local bodega in Harlem that is rumored to have created the now famous, Chopped Cheese sandwich. Camron often spoke about his life in NYC. I have always been fond of Hip Hop and rap from NYC. I felt like I was being transported to a different part of the world when I listened to Hip Hop from different parts of the world. Camron is part of a group called The Diplomats. The Diplomats rep Harlem through and through. If it's popular or in style in Harlem, The Diplomats speak or have spoken on it! I recently visited NYC and saw a Chopped Cheese sandwich featured on a menu in a Bodega. I had never actually seen a Chopped Cheese and internally geeked out that I was seeing something that I had only heard about in rhyme.

Recently  "Jim Jones" a member of the Diplomats released a video called "Chicken Fried Rice"  The video goes into a cut scene that features guest rapper "Yo Gotti"(not a member of The Diplomats) ordering a Chopped Cheese sandwich. It was at this point, I knew I needed to put my version of the Chopped Cheese sandwich in my book. I came up with this recipe based on the research I've done on this NYC bodega favorite sandwich. I wanted to pay homage to the sandwich without bastardizing the original. Like all recipes in this book, I am only giving you my interpretation. I feel that this sandwich is a classic that should be enjoyed by more people. I know that this Chopped Cheese recipe is already one of my go-to's for a great sandwich! I hope you enjoy. Shout out to Harlem, NYC and The Diplomats AKA DIPSET!

This is how my last chopped cheese looked. I get hungry every time I see these pictures!

# Chopped Cheese

1/2 pound 80/20 ground beef ( or 2 1/4 pound patties)

A few slices of bacon (cut up)

1 small onion

Lettuce

1 tomato

2 slices of cheese (I use mild or sharp cheddar)

Mayonnaise

Ketchup

Mustard

Season Salt

12 inch hero roll (sub sandwich roll)

1. Chop your onions, lettuce, and bacon and set aside. Thinly slice your tomato. I normally use 3-4 slices of tomato, but the size of your bread will help you determine how many you need.

2. Heat a large skillet to medium high heat. Place onions and bacon in skillet and sauté until the bacon and onions are caramelized. Remove cooked items and place in dish for future use.

3. Add beef to the same skillet you cooked the bacon and onions in. Chop* beef with one or two heavy duty spatulas. Once meat is about half way cooked, add season salt, and the onions and bacon that were cooked earlier. Continue to cook/chop your mixture until the beef is fully cooked. Scrape all of the mixture to one side of the pan, add cheese on top and remove from the heat.

4. Spread a small amount of butter on both sides of your roll. Use a panini press(or toast on both sides with a broiler) to grill bun. Once bun is toasted, cut in half and add a thin layer of mayonnaise inside. Add mustard and ketchup to both sides. Use spatula to scoop all of the contents from your skillet into your bun. Place chopped lettuce and sliced tomatoes on top of the chopped beef. Close sandwich and cut in half. If you want to experience your sandwich the way you would in a bodega, wrap it in wax paper before you cut it in half. The wax paper will also help keep your sandwich warm.

\* The "chop" that I am referring to is the motion you should use to cook your beef. I hold my spatulas sideways and use a knifelike chop to cook/cut the beef, onion and bacon.

I originally joined the military so I could travel the world. I was upset when I was at technical training school the day we received our first duty assignments! My "dream sheet" of places I wanted to go were all overseas. I ended up getting an assignment to Cannon Air Force in New Mexico. I was pissed! Luckily for me there was a guy in my class that didn't want to leave the states. I was able to swap my assignment with his and just like that, I had an assignment to Kadena Air Force base in Okinawa, Japan. I was adventurous with food before I moved to Okinawa, but I really started to develop my love for different cuisines when I moved there. The people in Okinawa are so friendly and I learned a lot of patience from watching and observing their culture. The food on Okinawa is similar to the food on mainland Japan, but it has its own signature taste.

One of my favorite dishes that I use to eat while I was stationed on Kadena was taco rice! Taco rice is rumored to have been invented on Okinawa. I've never seen it on a menu anywhere outside of Japan. I normally only ate this dish after a long night of clubbing. Taco rice was one of the dishes that was served at the bowling alley on base that gave you the best bang for your buck. Not only was this dish packed with flavor, it was also a huge portion! The concept might sound weird, but if you like tacos and you like rice, then you will love taco rice. This dish is prepared differently based on where you go to eat it, but I think the version that was made at the bowling alley on base is the best! I recently traveled back to Okinawa and I ordered some so that I could try to replicate this simple but delicious dish. I love the way a meal can take you on a mental journey. It's almost like the flavors and smells can transport you back to a memory that might have been fading away. I have a lot of good memories associated with the Island of Okinawa, and many of them involved the unique cuisine offered there.

# Taco Rice

1 pound of ground beef

1 1/2 cups of rice

1 packet of taco season

Diced tomatoes

Shredded cheese (Taco Blend)

shredded lettuce

Salsa (optional)

1.  Cook rice in accordance with instructions on your bag of rice. I prefer to use sushi style rice because it gets sticky when it's cooked.

2.  While your rice is cooking, prepare ground beef based on the directions on your packet of taco seasoning. Keep warm.

3.  Dice your tomato and shred your lettuce if it isn't already done.

4.  Place about a cup or so of rice on a plate and top with taco meat, cheese, lettuce and tomato. You can top with salsa, sour cream, or guacamole. There really isn't any rules when it comes to how you want to dress your taco rice. For best results serve while your rice and meat are still warm.

*I took the above picture last time I was visiting Okinawa. It was nice to have a nostalgic dish, but I feel my recipe will help fill the void and introduce people to this classic dish.*

# Beef Enchiladas*

**1 pound of ground beef (or Barbacoa meat from recipe)**

**1 small can of green chilies (drained)**

**1 package of corn tortillas**

**1 medium onion (diced)**

**1 pack of taco seasoning of your choice**

**2 cans of enchilada sauce (green or red sauce will work)**

**1 tsp of diced garlic**

**1 bag of Mexican cheese**

**Canola oil**

1. Sauté onions in a medium size skillet over medium heat. Once onions are starting to become translucent and soft, add in ground beef. Cook ground beef in accordance with taco seasoning pack (If you are using barbacoa instead of ground meat, add here). Once you have drained the fat from the meat, stir in garlic, season pack, chilies and any liquid required from the season pack instructions. Continue to cook until complete based on instructions. Add a handful of cheese and a small amount of enchilada sauce to the meat mixture, stir and set aside. Pre heat oven to 350 degrees F.

2. In a small pot, bring Enchilada sauce to a simmer and remove from heat.

3. Heat a shallow amount of oil in a small pan. Once the oil comes up to heat, you will need to briefly fry each corn tortilla on both sides. If you skip this step, the tortillas will break or crumble when you try to add filling to them.

4. Arrange tortillas in a 13x9 inch casserole dish. You should have enough room to have 3 or 4 across (once rolled) for two or 3 rows. Spoon an even amount of meat mixture into each tortilla. Sprinkle a bit of cheese on top of the meat and close tortilla in a cylinder shape. Roll tortilla over so that the seams are facing down. Continue process until all of your tortillas have been filled or you have exhausted your meat filling supply.

5. Pour enchilada sauce over the tortilla's. Cover tortillas with a generous amount of cheese. Place casserole into the oven and cook until the sauce has started to bubble and all the cheese is nicely melted.

6. I like to serve this dish with a little sour cream and hot sauce.

* I ate a lot of Tex-Mex food when I lived in San Antonio. Back then, I thought all Mexican food was the same. I later learned that food from Mexico was way different than the food I grew eating in Texas. This recipe is far from an authentic Mexican recipe! This recipe is my take on one of my favorite dishes. Some people only like to eat food cooked the traditional way. One of the things I loved about eating at Tex-Mex restaurants, (in Texas) was the different flavors and approaches on the same dish. I feel like I came up with a nice balance of all of my favorite ways to eat enchiladas. I hope you all enjoy this recipe as much as I do.

# Beef Enchiladas

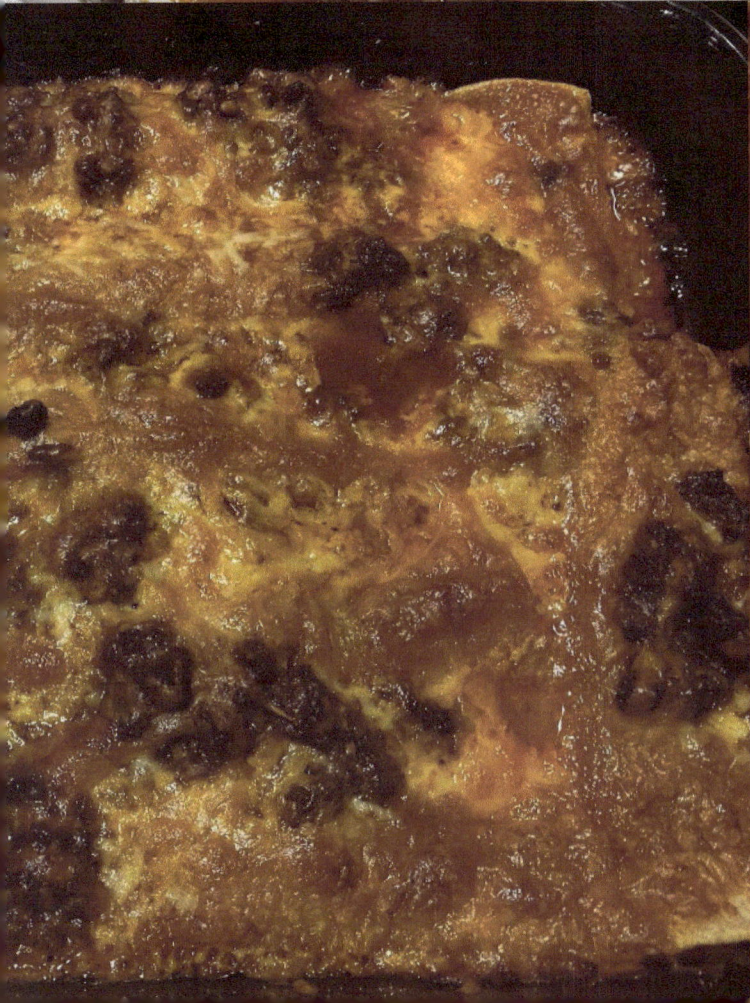

# Shrimp and Grits

# Shrimp and Grits

The first time I ever had shrimp and grits I was in South Carolina. We moved to South Carolina when I was a kid because my dad had gotten reassigned to Fort Jackson in Columbia, SC. Food is heavily celebrated in the Carolina's! I love when I have a chance to visit family in South Carolina because I know I will have a good time and I know I will eat well!

My Shrimp and Grits recipe is my take on Southern style shrimp and Grits. I've had Shrimp and Grits prepared many ways and this recipe combines what I like most from the different styles I've had. I hope you enjoy as much as I do!

Ingredients

1/2 to 1 pound of raw shrimp

32 ounces of seafood stock

Green onions (normal bushel)

2 bell peppers

1 large yellow onion

1 ear of corn

1 Andouille sausage

1/4 pound of thick cut bacon (cubed)

3/4 cup of white grits (preferably from the Carolina's)

2 Tbsp all purpose flour

3 cups of whole milk

1 1/2 cups of shredded sharp cheddar cheese

 Salt, Pepper and Creole seasoning to taste

1 Tbsp chopped garlic

1. Before you start cooking you should chop all of your ingredients that will need chopping so that you don't have to stop in the middle of cooking. With that being said, you need to chop your peppers(save the core and excess) and yellow onions. There isn't a right or wrong way to chop but make sure you cut your vegetables small enough so that they evenly cook. Chop your green onions and make sure you save the roots. Cut your Andouille sausage (about a 1/4 inch thick) at an angle. Remove the husk and silk from your ear of corn. Cut the kernels off your corn and place it aside with the rest of your prepared items.

2. If you have shells on your shrimp, you will need to remove the shells and de-vein the shrimp. If you bought your shrimp peeled and de-veined you will only need to remove the shell from the tail. Place peeled shells you have in a pot with stock, green onion roots, and pepper cores. Cook stock over low heat for 10-15 minuets. Strain contents of pot into a large bowl. Your stock should be free of any of the additional items you put in your pot. Set aside for now.

3. Place your Sausage and bacon cubes in a large skillet over medium high heat. Cook meat until it has a nice sear on all sides. I like to cook until the bacon is almost crispy. Transfer meat to a bowl or plate and make sure you retain the juices in your pan.

4. Sauté all of the vegetables (excluding garlic) you cut in the large skillet. You want to sauté your vegetables until they start to caramelize but not burn. You might need to add a tablespoon of butter or two to keep vegetables from sticking. Times will vary depending on the size of your vegetables you have prepared. Once your vegetables are sautéed add in your garlic and cook for another few minutes. I add the garlic last because it tends to pop off the pan if you cook it too early. Stir in flour and try to distribute throughout the pan. Be sure to keep stirring until all flour has been cooked through. Add about a cup of your stock to your vegetables. The stock will deglaze your pan. Slowly add the rest of your stock and the meat you cooked to your vegetables and cook until your sauce starts to thicken.

5. Bring milk to a rolling boil and add grits. Reduce heat and continue to monitor and stir grits. I like to add a little butter and salt to my grits while they are cooking. Once your grits have cooked to your desired consistency pull from heat and stir in shredded cheese.

6. Fry shrimp over medium high heat until they have cooked through. I use a tablespoon of butter and some creole seasoning when I fry my shrimp.

7. Place your cheesy grits in a bowl and top with vegetable/meat mix. Top with some of your shrimp and garnish with diced tomatoes and a sprinkle of creole seasoning

# Fishing For Tacos

Living in Florida has given me plenty of opportunities to go fishing. I'm not much of a go to the beach and sit around type of guy. When I go to the beach, I enjoy fishing. Surf fishing is challenging because there are so many variables. On a good day, I can walk away with enough fish to make fresh fish tacos. I think the tacos taste better when you catch and harvest the fish yourself!

# Fish >━━❭ Tacos

**2-4 boneless white fish filets**

**2-4 Flour tortillas**

**Shredded lettuce**

**Kewpie (Japanese Mayonnaise)**

**Shredded cheese**

**Avocado (cut into slices or small chunks)**

**Mango salsa**

**Preferred seasoning**

**1 small lime (cut in half)**

1. Season fish with any seasoning of your choice. Salt and pepper work fine but sometimes I like to add Cajun or blackened seasoning.

2. Add a tablespoon of butter or olive oil to a medium skillet over medium heat. Heat until the butter or oil is hot enough to fry. Be sure to swirl the oil in the pan to ensure there are no dry spots.

3. Fry fish until you get a nice crisp char on both sides. Once the fish looks white and flaky it is done. Squeeze the juice of half of the lime into the pan. The lime juice will help deglaze some of the seasonings from the pan. Transfer fish and pan juices to a plate. Cut fish into small chunks.

4. Heat a large skillet over medium high heat. Place a tortilla on the skillet and cook each side for about 30-40 seconds. Repeat with as many tortillas that you decide to cook.

5. To assemble the tacos :

- place a small amount of shredded lettuce on the top of each tortilla

- Place avocado pieces on top of lettuce

- squeeze a small amount of Kewpie on top of the avocado

- Put fish, cheese and salsa on tortilla.

6. Tacos are best served immediately. I like to use the remaining lime half to squeeze over the tacos as I eat them.

# Chicken Katsu

The first time I tasted Chicken Katsu was when I was stationed in Okinawa, Japan. A lot of people on the island talked up this place called CoCo's. The actual name is "Curry House CoCo ICHIBANYA" but folks just called it CoCo's. I ignored all the talk about this place for a while. One reason I put off going to CoCo's was because I was broke half of the time and I didn't always have money to go out to eat. Once I finally went, I was hooked! I asked my friend what I should get and he told me to get the chicken curry with rice. I never ate anything else when I went there! It was always the chicken curry for me. I knew I liked the chicken and I didn't feel the need to potentially waste my money on another dish that I didn't like.

The last time I was in Okinawa, I went to CoCo's with my wife and a few friends. I was willing to be a little more adventurous this time around. I ordered the Beef,Pork and Chicken curry meal with garlic and cheese Naan bread. The beef and the pork was just as good as the chicken! Currently the only states you can get Coco's in the United States are Hawaii and California. Most people I speak to have never heard of CoCo's. A lot of places have chicken katsu, but I like the way that CoCo's pairs theirs with curry. I tried to come as close as I can to recreating CoCo's recipe for at home cooks. My recipe is just my take on what they make. Nothing beats the original but I like what I came up with. The below pictures are from my last trip to Okinawa.

# Chicken Katsu Curry

1 medium onion sliced thin

I large or two medium sized carrot

4 slices of maple bacon sliced (optional)

1/2 cup of beef stock

2 cups of water

1 tsp of white vinegar

1 tsp of Worcestershire sauce

Salt & Pepper

2 tbsp of butter

1 lb of sliced chicken breast (Scaloppini Style)

1 1/2 cups of sushi style rice (I use Nishiki)

Vegetable oil (enough to cover the bottom of a medium size skillet)

2-3 large eggs

Flour

Panko

2 blocks of curry from a 3.2 oz box of Golden Curry

1 tsp of curry powder

1. Slice onions and carrot into thin slices. Place butter into a medium size sauce pot over medium heat.  Add in onions and carrot slices and sauté until tender and caramelized.

2.  Add sliced bacon into the pot and cook until bacon starts to caramelize. Add in two cups of water and deglaze the pot , making sure you stir in all of the items that may be stuck to the bottom or side of the pot. Cook mixture for about 5 additional minutes at a slow boil.

3.  Remove pot from heat. Use an immersion blender to blend the items in the pot together.  The mixture should be smooth. It's ok to have a few small chucks but the overall consistency should be smooth.

4. Put the pot back on medium heat. Add beef stock, salt and pepper to taste, vinegar, Worcestershire sauce, curry powder and blocks of golden curry.  Stir all items together and continue to cook over low heat. Make sure you taste your curry mixture to make sure it has the taste that you want. If you would like your curry to be spicier, you should use the "hot" golden curry blocks.  Keep curry warm until ready to serve.

# Chicken Katsu Curry

5. Assemble your breading station:

- Spread out flour on a plate or dish

- Beat 2-3 eggs in a large bowl

- Spread out Panko on a plate or dish

6. Clean chicken and season with your favorite seasoning. I like to keep it simple with this recipe. I sprinkle my chicken with garlic powder, salt, pepper and paprika.

7. Dip each piece of chicken in the flour, egg and Panko (in that order). All exposed surface of the chicken should be covered with breading.

8. Heat vegetable oil in a large skillet over medium hot heat. While the oil is heating up, place the rice in a pot or rice cooker and follow in instructions on the bag.

9. Place chicken in skillet and fry on both sides. Make sure the chicken is cooked all the way through. The chicken should be golden brown and crispy. Use an instant read thermometer if you are unsure if the chicken is cooked thoroughly.

10. Make sure that you properly drain the chicken after you remove it from the frying pan. I like to place the chicken on a wire rack, so that the oil that is still on the chicken has room to drip. If you fail to properly drain the chicken, it might have excess oil buildup on the bottom of the cutlet.

11. Once all of your chicken is fried and your rice is done, it's time to assemble your plate.

12. Place some of the rice on a plate and place a sliced piece of chicken on top of the rice. Pour some of the warm curry over some of the chicken. Make sure you put enough curry on your plate so that you have enough to dip and mix the chicken and rice with.

13. Naan bread goes well with this dish! You can also use the method in this recipe to cook pork or beef cutlets. I hope you enjoy this dish as much as I do!

# Braised Oxtail

Oxtails rarely get the praise they deserve in my opinion! My mom and dad made oxtails every once in a while when I was a kid, but I didn't really start to like Oxtails until I started ordering them from Jamaican and Caribbean spots. When I first moved to Florida, I met a Jamaican barber when I went to get my hair cut. He is a great barber, so I continued to go back and get my hair cut. After a few months in his chair, we started to talk about other things beside current events and what not.

One day I asked him if he knew how to cook any Jamaican food. His response was, "WHAT" You already know Pa( slang for a man or guy)! I asked him what was one of his favorite things to make? Oxtails was one of the things he mentioned! I was like, "oh snaps" I love Oxtails! I told him about a local spot that I go to to get them and he was like those Oxtails can't touch mine! I was intrigued! I wanted to know how he cooked his, because I like the ones from the spot I told him about. After a few more hair cuts, he started to give me some of the ingredients that he uses when he cooks his Oxtails. Armed with the information I got from him, I took to the internet to try to make sense of the breadcrumbs he dropped. I attempted to to make my own after some research. I remembered he said that he served his oxtails with rice

and peas. When my oxtails were close to finishing, I made some rice and cooked some green peas. I was proud of my creation so a snapped a bunch of pictures. Next time I went to get my hair cut ,I took my phone out to show my barber my creation! He was like, "ohhhhh I see you Son, doing your thing!" He said the oxtails looked good but asked me what was in the rice? I said peas! You said you cooked them with rice and peas right? Next thing I know, he let out one of the loudest laughs! I said, WHAT'S SO FUNNY?

He said "when I said peas, I really meant kidney beans"! I was pissed! I said, well how in the hell am I supposed to know that? We both had a laugh about whole situation. I have changed the recipe up a few times to make it my own. The wine and the stock was something that I added recently to my recipe. I also used different seasoning over the years, but I'm happy with the recipe I wrote. I encourage you to make your own variation of my recipe to suit your taste buds! Cooking is all about experimenting and variations!

# Braised Oxtail

3 lbs of Oxtail (beef cow tail)

2 medium sized sweet onions (sliced)

3-4 bushels of green onions

1-2 cups of sliced bell pepper

32 ounces of beef stock

6 cloves of garlic (peeled and sliced)

1 scotch bonnet pepper (optional and also known as habanero)

1 sweet potato (peeled and diced)

1 cup of red wine

Sea salt

1 tsp of fresh ground black pepper

1 tsp of Paprika

2 tsp of Vegeta (or any vegetable based seasoning)

1 tsp Gravy Master (or Kitchen Bouquet, browning & seasoning sauce)

1.   Clean Oxtails and separate/cut into the size that you would like to cook. I like to add a little white vinegar or lemon juice to the water that I rinse and wash the Oxtails in.  Pat the oxtails with a napkin until they are dry.

2.   Place Oxtails in a large sealable container or bowl. Add Gravy Master and make sure that it comes in contact with all of the Oxtails. You might have to move the Oxtails around to ensure that they are properly covered.  Season Oxtails with Salt, Pepper, Paprika, & Vegeta. Make sure that you coat all sides of the Oxtails.

3.   Place Garlic, bell pepper,  green onions, sweet potato, onions and scotch bonnet in the container and give a light mix. Make sure you do not tear the scotch bonnet. The seeds of the scotch bonnet peppers are very hot and you don't want them to over power the taste of this dish.

4.   Place the container with the Oxtails in the refrigerator for 10-24 hours. I like to shake or stir the contents of the container 2-3 times while its in the refrigerator. You want to make sure that the contents are properly mixed.

5.   Remove the container from the refrigerator and let it sit at room temperature for about 20 minutes. Heat 2-3

tablespoons of oil over medium high heat in a large pot or dutch oven. Separate Oxtails from all of the other items that are in the container.

6.   Sear Oxtails on all sides until you get a nice crust on each one. You don't have to worry about cooking the oxtails all the way through. At this point we are only trying to lock in the flavor. Once browned, remove and set the oxtails to the side.

7.   Add remaining contents from the container you used to marinade the Oxtail into the pot. Cook until the vegetables start to sauté. Add the oxtails that you set aside, beef stock, and red wine. Cover the dutch oven or pot and reduce heat to medium low.

8.   Cook contents in your pot for 2-3 hours . Check every once in a while to ensure nothing is sticking to the pot. Cooking times vary based on the type of stove you are using and the size of your oxtails. You will know the oxtails are done, when you are able to easily pull the meat away from the bone of the oxtail with a fork.

# Braised Oxtail

I like to serve the oxtails with rice, mash potatoes or pasta. The last time I cooked this dish, I separated the meat from the bones once everything was done cooking and mixed some of the meat and vegetables with Alfredo pasta. Oxtails don't often get the respect that I think they deserve. If you are a fan of beef, I think that you won't be disappointed with this recipe!

# Sweet Thangs

# Chapter 5
# Sweet Thangs

Sweets have always played a major role in my life. I would like to say I could live without sweets or that they don't matter that much to me, but I would be lying. I was blessed to have great bakers in my family. My grandmothers kept fresh pies and cakes in their house for when we used to visit. It was almost a right of passage of going to both my grandmothers houses.

My mom and dad also liked to make sweets. I'll never forget the day when my father came back from being in "The Field" for a few weeks with his Army unit. He had our whole kitchen turned into a donut making assembly line. You would have thought you were walking into a legit donut shop! The look on his face when he saw how excited I was, was priceless! You see, my connection with sweets go beyond the ingredients that it takes to make them. My connections with sweets are based off of a feeling that I have or had that connects me to enjoying a slice of cake, a piece of Baklava or a glazed donut.

I tried to cut sweets out of my life for a few months. I was able to do it and didn't really crave any after the first two weeks. I felt like my diet lacked balance without sweets. I didn't need sweets but I did want them. These days, I try to balance out how many sweets I eat. There are times where I get a sweet-tooth and I feel like I need to have a dessert every other day. Then there are times where I go weeks without anything sweet.

In this chapter I will share a few of my go to desserts, AKA "sweet thangs". I am constantly looking for my next go to sweet thang. Few desserts give me the emotional connections that the ones my grandmothers use to make, but searching for them is both fun and delicious!

# SWEET THANGS

PECAN PIE

BAKLAVA

AÇAÍ BOWL

GRILLED PINEAPPLES

SALTED CARAMEL
COGNAC ICE-CREAM

COGNAC GLAZED PEACH
TURNOVERS

# Pecan Pie

1 cup light corn syrup

1 cup of vanilla infused sugar(see the end of this chapter for this recipe)

3 organic free range eggs

2 tablespoons of melted butter

1 tsp bourbon vanilla extract

1 1/2 cups of shelled and halved pecans

1 deep dish pie crust( home made or store bought)

1.  Place eggs in a large bowl and mix until egg yokes are fully mixed in. Add sugar, butter, corn syrup and vanilla extract to eggs and thoroughly mix.

2.  Add pecan to your mixture and gently stir with a big spoon. Makes sure that you don't over stir at this stage because you don't want to break the pecans.

3.  Pour contents into a frozen or fresh deep dish pie crust. I have always made this pie with a store bought deep dish pie crust. If you have a trusted homemade pie crust you could definitely use it for this recipe, but I like the taste of the store-bought brand that I have used for years.

4.  Place pie into a preheated oven set to 350 degrees F.

5.  Set a timer for 1 hour once you put your pie in the oven. At the one hour mark you will need to start to monitor your pie. If you pull the pie too early, your pie will be runny. If you leave the pie in too long, then your pie will burn. I feel that the sweet spot is when the pie is sort of firm to the touch snd the pecans start to rise slightly and show a somewhat firm interior. All ovens cook differently and it is best to monitor after the one hour mark. Most times, my pies are done anywhere between 65-80 minutes in the oven. The top of my pies normally have a deep bourbon appearance when they are done.  Let pie cool for around two hours. This pie is best served with whipped cream or vanilla ice cream.

# Baklava

The first time that I ever had Baklava was in a small Turkish kebab shop in Speicher, Germany. I lived a few miles away from the Kebab shop and everyone told me it was the best place to go for food in the area. I went to the shop an average of about once a week the whole time I was stationed at Spangdahlem. When I first started going in, I would order the same thing(Large toasted Kebab with goat cheese, spice, lettuce, tomato, red onion, & garlic cream sauce).

One day I saw a guy ask for some baklava. I'd seen the baklava before but I never really knew what it was so I ignored it. I asked the guy making my order what the baklava is and was it good? The guy looks at me with a dead stare and he said, "buddy, you never had baklava"? I said, "no, I never heard of it"! He said, you have to try! I asked him what it was and he said it was pastry with nuts and honey(a real Turkish delicacy). I honestly was thrown off because every time I had seen the baklava before it was covered with specs of green. I didn't know that the specs were chopped up pieces of pistachios. I also thought that it was such a small dessert, that it couldn't be that satisfying. I was wrong! I was pleasantly surprised! I couldn't believe that small piece of pastry packed that much flavor! The first time I had it, it tasted sort of like pecan pie. Pecan pie is the closest thing I can compare it to on a flavor profile.

I've seen baklava in many places through out my travels. I never questioned the origin of the dish because I was introduced to the dish from a Turkish man that said it was a Turkish dish. A few years ago I was invited to a Greek festival by one of my former students. He told me there would be Greek food and dancing, so I decided to go check it out. I was surprised to see baklava at one of the booths that was selling desserts. I purchased a few of the Greek deserts. When I ran into my student I told him I had purchased a couple pieces of baklava and said 'I am surprised that they are selling a Turkish dessert at a Greek festival". Why did I say that? He said, " You do know that the Greeks invented Baklava"? I was confused! I did some research online and noticed that the history of baklava is tricky! I spoke to my student more in depth about the situation and I told him that I wanted to attempt to make the dish, so I could add it to my cook book. He said it should be made the Greek way so he would assist me with some help from some of his family members. I ended up getting some reference recipes from him and some guidance on how to handle the filo dough. I feel that my baklava recipe pays homage to the dessert that I have grown to love. I like both the Turkish and Greek versions of the dish. I hope that you attempt to make this dish. I know it has a lot of steps, but the end result is worth it!

# Baklava

**1 lb of fillo dough (1 box thawed out in the refrigerator overnight)**

**3 sticks of unsalted butter**

**1 lb walnuts**

**1/2 Lb of almonds**

**1 tsp nutmeg**

**2 tsp allspice**

**2 tsp cinnamon**

**Whole cloves**

**1 tsp bourbon vanilla extract**

**1/2 cup sugar (vanilla infused works great on this recipe)**

**Syrup:**

**3 cups of Sugar**

**2 cups of water**

**1 stick of Cinnamon**

**4 cloves**

**1 tsp of fresh lemon juice**

**2 tbsp of local honey**

1. Combine walnuts, almonds, cinnamon, allspice, nutmeg and vanilla in a food processor. Chop until everything is nicely blended. You don't want the nuts in the mixture to be too big but you also don't want them to be over chopped.

2. Heat butter in a small pan until all butter is melted. Set aside. Place fillo on a wax paper and cover with another piece of wax paper. Cover fillo with a damp cloth. The cloth will help keep your fillo from drying out while you assemble your baklava.

3. Brush the bottom of a large baking pan with some of the melted butter. I like to use a large round pan for presentation purposes.

4. Line the bottom of your pan with 12 fillo, brushing each layer with butter before placing on a new layer. This is your base layer. The fillo will be delicate, so make sure you are careful when you handle it.

5. Sprinkle base layer of fillo with a thin layer of nut mixture. Cover with 3 layers of fillo, and make sure you brush each layer with butter. You will repeat the process in this step until all of your nut mixture is used. It will probably be 4 or five more layers. Once you have used all of your nut mixture, cover with 10 buttered fillo. At this point you need to chill your baklava in a refrigerator for about 30 minutes.

6. This is a good time to make the syrup: combine sugar, water, cinnamon stick, and 4 cloves in a small sauce pan. Bring to a slow simmer and let cook for about 10 min. Turn heat off and stir in honey. Let syrup cool. Strain syrup, so there won't be any pieces of clove or cinnamon stick left behind.

7. Remove chilled baklava from the refrigerator and cut dough into small diamond shapes. One of the reasons I like to use a round pan is because it's easier to cut. After you finish cutting your baklava, brush again with melted butter. Place a whole clove into the center of each large cut of the baklava( as pictured on previous page). Pre heat oven to 350 degrees F.

8. Bake baklava in oven for 1 hour. Your baklava should be golden brown when it is ready to come out of the oven.

9. After you remove the baklava from the oven, you need to ladle the syrup over it. Keep pouring syrup over the baklava until it has fully absorbed it. Try not to over saturate. You should be able to see when the baklava has stop absorbing the syrup.

10. Let baklava sit at room temperature for about an hour before serving. Be sure to remove cloves from the baklava before serving.

# Açaí Bowl

2 unsweetened Açaí pouches 100g each (normally 4 in a bag)

Half of a large ripe banana

1/2 cup of frozen mixed berries

1/4 cup of granola

Honey(local if available)

Chia seeds(optional)

Fresh fruit (chopped)

1/4 cup of juice, or milk (nut, oat or cow)

1.  Place Açaí pouches in warm water to partial thaw them out.

2.  Cut your preferred fruit into edible cuts and set aside.

3.  Pour contents of the Açaí pouches into a blender. Put banana, juice or milk, and frozen mixed berries into blender and blend until smooth.

4.  Pour blended mixture into a bowl. Arrange fruit on top of Açaí mix. Sprinkle granola and chia seeds on top. Finally, drizzle honey over the top of the contents of the bowl.

5.  This bowl is best when served immediately. The thing that I like the most about this dish is the way it can be easily modified to suit the needs of who is eating it.

# Grilled Pineapples

1 Whole Pineapple(cored and sliced) or 1-2 large cans of pineapple slices

1/4 cup of brown sugar

1 tsp of ground cinnamon

1 ounce of bourbon or whiskey (optional)

**Preheated BBQ grill**

1.  Mix sugar, cinnamon and bourbon in a large bowl.

2.  Place pineapple slices in bowl and make sure you cover all of the pineapples evenly with the sugar mixture.

3.  Let pineapples sit in the bowl for at least 15 minutes.

4.  Place pineapples over direct fire on the grill. Grill each pineapple for 2-3 minutes per side. It's cool if the pineapples get a nice char but be sure not to let them burn. The alcohol and the sugar should give the pineapples a nice deep brown crust.

5.  Once the pineapples are cooked, move them out of direct heat. I like to serve them warm, topped with a scoop or two of vanilla ice cream.

# SALTED CARAMEL COGNAC ICE CREAM

**2 cups of whole milk**

**1 1/4 cups of heavy cream**

**4 tsp. cornstarch**

**2/3 cup of sugar**

**2 tbsp Golden Syrup**

**1/4 tsp sea salt**

**3 tbsp cream cheese (room temp)**

**2 chocolate butter toffee candy bars 1.4 ounce each**

**1/4 cup cognac**

**1 vanilla pod**

**1/4 tsp of Xanthan gum (optional)**

**Sea salt caramel 2-4 ounces**

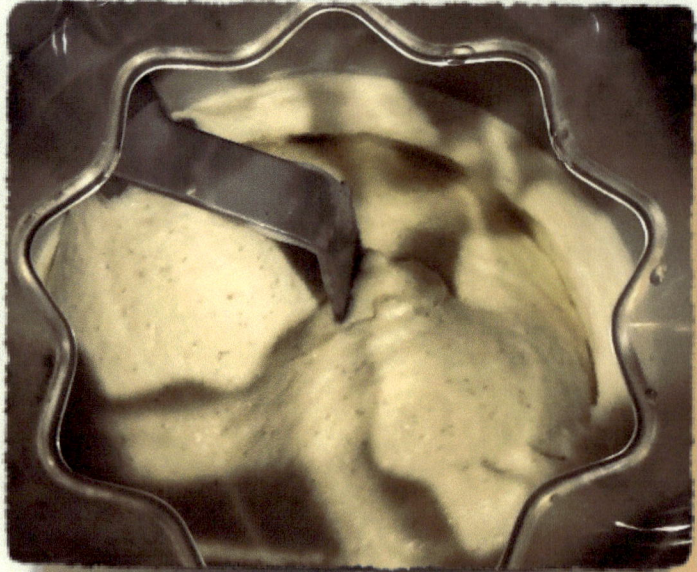

1.  Slice vanilla pod open and scrap beans from both sides of the pod. The beans will look like a small amount of black paste. The individual beans will be more visible once they are mixed in liquid.

2.  Mix 1/4 cup of milk with cornstarch. This mixture will serve as a thickening agent for your ice cream base.

3.  In a large sauce pan combine 1 3/4 cup of milk, salt, cream, sugar, xanthan gum(optional), Golden Syrup and scraped vanilla pod with beans. Let mixture come to a low boil over medium heat. After mixture has boiled for a few minutes, mix in cornstarch mixture with a wire whisk. Cook mixture until it it begins to thicken. You will feel the mixture thicken as you stir it with the wire whisk. It's imperative that you don't let the mixture cook too long. You don't want the milk to scorch in the process of thickening the mixture!

4.  Remove mixture from the heat. Pour a small amount of the mixture through a wire mesh strainer into a large bowl with the cream cheese. Mix until the cream cheese is well integrated, and then strain the remaining liquid in and mix well. Whisk in cognac and transfer to a clean sealable container. I like to let the mixture chill in the refrigerator overnight to allow time for all of the flavors in the mixture to marry.

5.  If you have an ice cream maker that requires you to freeze the bowl, you want to make sure your bowl has been in the freezer for well over 24 hours. The last thing you want is for your bowl to get warm while your ice cream is churning.

# SALTED CARAMEL COGNAC ICE CREAM

6. When you know your bowl is ready to make your ice cream and the base mixture has had adequate time to chill in the refrigerator, prepare your ice cream assembly.

7. Chop candy bars into small chunks. Make sure the sea salt caramel is at room temperature. If the caramel is too cold, it will be hard to mix when you are preparing the ice cream containers.

8. Set up ice cream maker in accordance with manufacture instructions.

9. Pour chilled ice cream base into ice cream maker and let churn until you reach the desired consistency. Right before you turn off the machine, pour in the candy pieces that you chopped. You don't need or want to over mix at this step in the process. Turn off the ice cream maker and prepare to assemble your container/containers.

10. To assemble the ice cream, start by drizzling a small ribbon of the salted caramel on the bottom of a pint size or quart sized container. Spoon on a layer of the ice cream and repeat the caramel drizzle step. Continue to alternate each step until you get near the top of the container. This recipe will make around two pint size containers or one quart sized containers. When you have reached the top of the container, cover the ice cream with a piece of parchment paper before putting on the lid. The parchment paper will help keep the container air tight.

When I decided to make a recipe for Ice cream, I asked myself "what I would like to have that I haven't seen on the market". I like Cognac but I normally only see Bourbon based Ice Creams. The salted caramel and the chocolate covered toffee bars take this recipe to another level! Feel free to add or change based on your preferences, but I think this is a must try recipe!

11. Place ice cream in the coldest part of your freezer. I like to let the ice cream harden for at least 8-10 hours before I serve or eat it.

12. The ice cream should keep well for a few weeks in the freezer. If you use Xanthan gum, the ice cream will be less likely to crystallize. This recipe is good on its own but it goes very well with my pecan pie recipe. I hope you enjoy it as much as I do!

# Peaches

My mother's family is from a small town in Georgia. Georgia is known as the peach state and I can remember eating peaches for as long as I've been alive.

My grandmother use to make all of us small peach filled pastries she called "peach puffs". It was a great treat and I remember me and all of my cousins rushing inside to grab a peach puff when they were finished cooking. I never got around to asking my grandmother how she made her peach puffs before she passed away. I feel that even if I did get the recipe from her, I doubt I would have shared it out of respect. I think it's crazy how some of my most memorable moments have some type of food tied to them.

I decided to try to recapture the essence of what my grandmother use to make with my own personal spin. What I came up with is my cognac glazed peach turnovers recipe. It's been over twenty years since I've had one of my grandmothers peach puffs, so it is hard to know if I hit the mark. When I took the first bite of my peach turnovers, I got a huge smile on my face. I feel that if my grandmother were still alive she would definitely approve of the recipe I came up with.

Georgia is known as the peach state and I am so thankful to my grandmother for providing me with a memory that incorporates peaches and her cooking skills! I hope that my cognac glazed peach turnover recipe can put a smile on your face, like it does mine.

# Cognac Glazed Peach Turnovers

**1 pack of thawed puff pastry sheets (I use the 17.3 oz Pepperidge Farm pack)**

**3 cups of frozen peaches**

**1 Tbsp of lime juice**

**1/4 tsp bourbon vanilla extract**

**2 TBSP butter**

**1/8 Cup sugar**

**1/8 cup of brown sugar**

**2 tsp cornstarch**

**1 egg**

**1 TBSP water**

**Sugar ( turbinado, raw or normal cane)**

**For optional Cognac Glaze:**

**1 TBSP cognac**

**1/3 cup of powdered sugar**

1. Place peaches, lime juice, extract, butter, sugar, cornstarch, and brown sugar into medium size pot over medium high heat. Cook for about 8-12 minutes. While the contents are cooking stir items and use a heat proof spatula to break peaches into small chunks. The liquid rendered from the peaches should thicken.

2. Cut each of the two puff pastry sheets into 4 equal parts. You might need to slightly roll out each of the pastry sheets in order to make it easier to fold the pastry over the filling.  Beat egg with water and set aside.  Pre heat oven to 350° F.

3. Spoon 2 TBSP of the peach mixture into the center of each of the pastry pieces.  Fold the pastry into a triangle shape and seal the edges with a fork.

4. Brush a thin layer of the egg wash over each of the sealed pastries. Sprinkle some sugar over each pastry. Place each pastry evenly spaced on a sheet pan lined with wax or parchment paper.  Put pastries into pre heated oven and cook until the are golden brown. Cook time should take about 25 minutes.

5. While pastries cook, combine cognac and powered sugar in a small bowl. Whisk until you have a liquid consistency. If you want the glaze to be thicker, add more powdered sugar a little at a time until you reach the desired thickness.

6. Remove pastries from the oven and let cool for about 10 minutes. Cover each pastry with some of the cognac glaze.

# Vanilla Infused Sugar

All of the cane sugar that I use in my home is vanilla infused. I like the flavor and the aromatic scent vanilla pods bring to normal cane sugar. The vanilla pods that I use are always opened up and the beans have been removed for use in other recipes. Vanilla pods can be expensive, so finding ways to get more use out of them is ideal. The flavor that vanilla pods bring to normal sugar can be an added bonus to your dessert recipes.

| Ingredient | Amount |
|---|---|
| Cane Sugar | 3-5 pound Bag |
| Vanilla Pod | 1 or 2 |

1. Place vanilla pod that has been opened and scraped* inside a sealable container.

2. Pour sugar into the container, seal the container, and then give the container a good shake.

3. It is normal to see a few black vanilla beans mixed in throughout your sugar.

* To scrape out a vanilla pod, you need to run the tip of a sharp knife down the center of the vanilla pod from top to bottom. Once you are able to open the vanilla pod, use the back of your knife to scrape the vanilla beans out of the pod. The beans will look like a black paste. If you add the vanilla beans to a liquid based recipe, (like ice cream) you will see the individual beans.

# Kitchen Essentials

A good pan or skillet is something that every cook needs in their kitchen arsenal. I started out with cheap pots and pans and I had some difficulty with some of my dishes. My advice is to invest in a good set of pots and pans if you are serious about cooking. There are different styles of pots and pans based on the type of cooking you plan on doing. I think if you can only have one pan, it should be cast iron! Cast iron is versatile and will last a lifetime if cared for.

A good sharp knife is an invaluable tool to have in your kitchen. For the best value, I recommend buying the best knife you can buy based on your budget. You don't need to buy one of those huge knife block sets. You want your knife to be comfortable and sharp for best results. A dull knife can be more dangerous than a sharp knife if handled incorrectly. Buy a steel or stone that will help keep your knife or knives sharp.

If you plan on doing any baking or marinading, a good set of bowls are a must! I like the stainless steel bowls because they are pretty much indestructible. You can typically find a set that are stackable, so you can save cabinet space. I think the best part about these bowls is the ease at which they can be cleaned.

Most recipes require measured amounts of ingredients. A quality set of measuring cups and spoons are an absolute must for any cook. I like the stainless steal cups and spoons because they are easy to keep clean and they won't stain. I also like to use glass measuring cups, because they typically have multiple measurement lines on either side of the cup. One side of the glass measuring cups has metric and the other side has standard.

# Acknowledgements

First and foremost I would like to thank God! I would also like to thank all the people that have encouraged me and pushed me to make this book a reality. When I first started to speak about the "concept" of this book it was just that, a concept. Everyone I spoke to, told me it was a great idea! Thank you to all of my family(especially my mom), friends, coworkers, students, and anyone else that encouraged me to write this book. I didn't think I would get as much support as I did! I really appreciate everyone for their feedback and well wishes!

# Thank You

Thank you to my lovely wife Lee for always supporting me in everything I do. When I mentioned that I wanted to write a cookbook, she was and has been my number one supporter. She has also been my number one food critic. I often ask her to taste test new recipes that I am trying out. She always provides constructive feedback and sometimes helps me come up with additions that will help my recipes. Thanks for always being there for me! Love You!

# About the Author

Shawn Miles is a retired Air Force Master Sergeant(MSgt). MSgt Miles Ret. is currently an AFJROTC instructor and has been since he retired from the Air Force. Cooking and traveling rank high on things that he loves to do with his family and friends. Highlighting the foods that he learned to cook from around the world (with his personal twist), is the basis of this cookbook.

www.ingramcontent.com/pod-product-compliance
Lightning Source LLC
Chambersburg PA
CBHW042016090426

42811CB00015B/1661

* 9 7 8 0 5 7 8 9 8 1 7 1 0 *